Be Not Afraid ... I Go Before You

Dedication

This book is dedicated to our loved ones
who have departed from this world.
We love you forever and trust
that your love and teachings
will live on in our lives and actions.

Imelda K Butler

Be Not Afraid ...
I Go Before You

A COLLECTION OF STORIES FILLED WITH LOVE, LOSS AND
HOPE, WRITTEN BY LOVED ONES WHO HAVE BEEN BEREAVED

CURRACH
PRESS

First published in 2011 by
CURRACH PRESS
55A Spruce Avenue, Stillorgan Industrial Park,
Blackrock, Co Dublin

Cover by Bill Bolger
Illustrations by Emer O Boyle
Origination by Currach Press
Printed in Ireland by Gemini International Limited

ISBN 978-1-85607-757-6

Contents

Acknowledgements

We acknowledge the heartfelt stories from our wonderful contributors. We acknowledge the pain you have experienced and your courage to delve deep within your emotional reserves to share your stories. Thank you for making this book possible. May it be a guide so others can learn and heal.

We acknowledge and thank our families and friends who have supported us in our grieving journeys and encouraged us along the way.

Thank you also to Brian Carthy for his unending encouragement, support and wisdom which was very much appreciated throughout the process.

We wish to express our gratitude to our young designer Lisa Sullivan and to Bill Bolger who both interpreted the concept superbly and designed a meaningful visual for the book.

A special thanks to Patrick O' Donoghue, our editor, whose dedication and attention to detail were superb in this his very first book. We also thank Michael Brennan and all at Currach Press for their efforts in bringing this book to the public.

Thank you Margaret Fogarty for your secretarial support in maintaining the details of the process.

A special thanks to Frances for her vision and to Peter who diligently dedicated hours to reviewing and editing the book, and to each member of my family for your encouragement along the way, and the many other people who have supported this labour of love.

Thank you to one and all for your ongoing support.

Oremus pro invicum – Let us pray for each other!

Introduction

There is no pain greater than that felt when a loved one dies. I can testify to this statement. I have never felt a deeper pain than when my partner, husband, *anamchara* and loved one died. The pain my two daughters and I shared as a family when John died suddenly was a shocking experience, the likes of which we never thought possible for any person to experience. We had never endured such inconsolable grief in our lives before this event. It was like our hearts were broken open and shredded to pieces.

Through that pain we were inspired to share our stories as a source of therapy for ourselves and to provide hope for other grieving people. Our daughters had never encountered the grief associated with the death of a loved one and there seemed to be no answers or explanation for the situation. The shock was traumatic and the loss was unbearable.

Based on a dream I had, we decided to share the journey to bring hope and consolation to people who are experiencing loss and bereavement. We collated the stories from people with varying backgrounds, themes and stories. This was done with the purpose of giving you, the reader, a reference on how others have experienced and coped with the tragic loss of loved ones; from those who can empathise with your situation. With that intent, we hope that these stories bring a sense of understanding to what is happening in your life.

I understand that each individual's grieving process is unique. It is my hope that these stories will be a source of consolation and comfort to those immersed in the grieving process. The act of sharing these heartfelt stories has also brought blessings and grace to the authors on their own grieving journeys. *Be Not Afraid … I Go Before You* is intended to let recently bereaved people see that the emotions, pain and reactions which they encounter in this horrific situation are natural and normal.

The following chapters tell stories from the heart and from an experiential perspective. The stories are told by parents, partners, siblings, children, families, friends and colleagues – all of whom have been bereaved. Each person tells the background to their relationship with the deceased person, the event, their reaction and their unique perspective on their situation.

The proceeds from the profits of this book will be donated to the *GRÁ* (Love, in Irish) Charity or, in English, 'Growth Reaching Africa'. This charity organisation was set up in 2008 by a group of Irish students, headed by our daughter Maria, to sponsor education and feeding campaigns to Kenya in Africa. My husband John was an advocate of the charity and as part of the memory of all our loved ones, it is fitting that we use the profits to bring life, education and food to the world. That way our contributions to the book will benefit others as we reach beyond our own pain to make a difference in the world.

Foreword

by Russell J. Watson Ed.D

This book is a remarkable work of thought, feeling, and emotion; written by many who have shared their stories of grief, the hard work of healing, and the letting go of fear. Even as we grieve, and even as we reach out to each other in grief, we lighten the burden of grief. Our joy when shared with others is doubled. Our grief when shared with others is halved. By listening to the grief of others, we help them process, and slightly lighten their load.

Grief is like a recording that needs to be played and played until no more sound comes out. For some people that can be a very, very long time. This tapestry of ideas was shared to me by Revd Don Marxhausen, one who has done excellent grief work throughout his lifelong and distinguished career. I value his words, and the comfort he's brought to many people across the country. I value the work that Imelda has done in compiling this book , which was inspired by the loss of her husband, John, who coached and counselled many professionals and businesses around the world.

On the cover of this book, we see a rose. A petal is lost from the rose, as a loved one is lost from our lives on earth. Without holding a rose in our hands we may call-up the memory banks of our minds to remember the fragrance of the rose, we may also recall the slight pain from the point of the thorns. So also as we observe the physical design of the rose, we see the broad petals and the twists and turns as the petals form to the center. Between the beauty of the flower and the potential pain of the thorns we have a choice: We can despair that the rosebush has thorns, or we can rejoice that the thornbush has roses!

This book brings a spirit of rejoicing even through the pain of grief and loss. A popular author named Isaiah reminds us that all flesh is grass, and the grass and flowers fade, but the strength and word of the Lord endures forever. More petals will drop from the rose, and more people in our lives will pass on and go before us. We want to be reassured and not be afraid.

This book brings us those words of loss, also words of hope and reassurance. It is a Blessing for those of us who have contributed our thoughtwork. We hope that it is a Blessing for you, our readers.

CHAPTER ONE

Partners' Stories

I will love you and honour you all the days of my life; to have and to hold, from this day forward, for better, for worse, for richer, for poorer, in sickness and in health, until death do us part.

Very few people contemplate the sad consequences of that promise on the day of their wedding. 'Forever and ever' is what we feel and want in our partnership.

The question is: is anyone ever prepared to let go of their loved one?

While we may not be enamoured with all the habits of our loved one, we certainly don't wish for a life without them or never ever wished them dead. How can we possibly prepare for the death of our loved one?

Whether we are encountered with a leadtime through illness or the death is sudden – death is death – death is a final goodbye.

Yet our loved one is still very present in who we are and what we do. We still love them and they still love us. Just because they are not with us physically, doesn't mean they are not with us. They are in our hearts and souls forever.

The following stories of life and love and death and suffering and grieving are spoken from the heart of each contributor. We hope you receive peace, hope and consolation in the passages of these stories written by loved ones whose partners have died.

A Great Life & Partnership Shared

John and I knew and shared our whole lives for more than thirty five years. We knew the emotions and feelings behind every thought of mind, every expression on face, every feeling of heart, indeed, every part of life for each other. We lived, worked, socialised, gardened, walked, holidayed together and loved every aspect of our lives together. We often joked and said we wouldn't change a single thing about each other.

Shortly after we met, we went to Boston, USA, for a summer. Towards the end of our stay, we took the Greyhound bus on a budget tour for thirty days and got to explore a lot of the USA. One of our favourite places was the Grand Canyon. We hiked down the steep trek, camped overnight on the Colorado River at the base and returned to the South Rim surface the following day.

We liked to challenge the *status quo* and were competitive by times. One example was on that trek down the Grand Canyon – we wanted to complete the trek in record time – so we cut the trail – and took a short cut – only to be ordered back on the track by the horse back wardens. In 1977 it was pretty remote in the Grand Canyon and when we returned thirty two years later in 2009, we weren't brave enough to hike down again – no, this time we just drove around the rim – a sign of our fitness, age and wisdom, perhaps.

We married in August 1980, with just about three weeks notice, because it fitted in with a conference we were attending in England. In those days you could do that kind of thing. Or maybe it was just us. We seemed to live our life at a fast pace, but we enjoyed it that way.

We set up our consulting business in 1989, and that was the beginning of a wonderful journey. From day one, we were certain that we were on the right road, doing the right thing and making a real difference. I recall in the very early days getting a photocopier on trial – delivered to our spare upstairs bedroom. It came on Friday and the representative couldn't believe how much copying was done on it when he returned on Monday to try selling it to us.

That was our first Business Management Consultancy Course (BMCC) – put together in our spare bedroom over a weekend. Today our business, Century Management, continues the work begun in our converted bedroom and incidentally we still use the same photocopier supplier.

We have had rich days and poor days, and as the saying goes we've had both but we enjoyed the rich days better.

When we were asked what our greatest achievements in life were, both of our responses, without needing a second thought, were: our two beautiful darling daughters Michelle and Maria. They have warmed our hearts with fun, laughter and humour and bring eternal happiness to us forever. They taught us to love in deeper more meaningful ways and have completed us as people and parents. They also taught us to be mature – sometimes they might even say: 'Grow up Mum & Dad.'

John and I loved holidaying together. We travelled quite a bit on business and always loved to combine these trips with a few days holiday. Our last trip was to Russia in early July 2010. We holidayed in Saint Petersburg and Moscow prior to a very successful international conference in Moscow.

Just two weeks later and two weeks before our thirtieth wedding anniversary, on a sunny Sunday Irish afternoon, John and I decided to do a bit of gardening before watching a Gaelic hurling match on TV. We both enjoyed sports, especially Gaelic football, hurling and rugby and could feast on it at weekends – winter for rugby and summer for Gaelic. One thing for certain was that we never disagreed about sports. There was never a disagreement about which channel to watch.

Anyway, at 2.00 p.m. on Sunday 25 July 2010, we decided to garden. As John deadheaded roses – picked the dead heads off the roses – he got stung by a wasp. He suffered anaphylactic shock and went from being perfectly healthy to being stone dead in approximately ten minutes right there beside me in our lush green garden on that tragic sunny Sunday afternoon.

This same garden had hosted the wonderful wedding reception of our daughter Maria and Geoffrey just seven weeks earlier. We had a perfect day on 5 June – everything and everyone was all so happy, so full of life.

Now watching the life drain from my husband's body, as the paramedics and doctor treated him, brought such agonising surreal shock and pain.

From the great high of the perfect wedding day – to the depth of sorrow of the darkest nightmare, in such a short time, was almost unbelievable.

Seeing all the same people back in our garden as had been there at the happy wedding celebration – only now like they were frozen – the life had been drained from them – was a very strange situation to comprehend. The sad faces and tear drenched eyes replacing the laughter, music, happy smiles and partying glamour.

John and I didn't have a perfect relationship, but we did have a great relationship and we truly loved each other and enjoyed each other's presence in our lives. We were happy together.

During the funeral days following John's death we were encapsulated into a vacuum – a bubble – of guidance and protection. It was like we were carried through the procedures – functioning and doing the right things – with our kitchen taken over by family and friends – who served more tea/coffee/triangle sandwiches and cakes than ever witnessed by mankind. The girls and I mostly occupied the 'family room' where John lay still, sober, cold in the coffin.

The girls and I chatted and decided to say our parting farewells to John during the church service. The total service for John was respectful, personal and meaningful. He would have liked that ... simple yet complete.

John was not a very religious man by his own admission but he had a natural Christian spirit of true goodness. He would say he could read at Mass but wasn't holy enough to be Eucharistic Minister ... he would say to me 'that is for you'. He often talked about how he admired how I could connect into Level 4 spirituality.

Level 4 is part of a business model we developed for explaining the stages of human life and work to clients in our business. If you can imagine the four levels are like four steps on a stairs. There are four levels of the human being: Level 1 – the hand to do work; Level 2 – the head to think and plan work; Level 3 – the heart – to emotionally connect; and Level 4 – the soul to spiritually connect. All aspects are important engagements for success as a person. Our challenge is to appropriately connect at all four levels.

An interesting thing happened as we drove out of the church car park after Mass on the day John died. John said to me: 'Who is your man who gets things?' I replied: 'Who? What?' Then it dawned on me: 'Oh, you mean Saint Anthony'. 'Yes', John replied.

Then John said: 'Because I put something away and I can't find it. I didn't want to say anything to worry you, but then I said I better tell you in case anything would happen to me.' At that point I dismissed it, not wanting to think about anything happening saying: 'Don't worry; sure we'll get it tomorrow.' Within three hours John was dead.

John's theme in life was 'live well, laugh often and leave a legacy'. As I said in 'Remembering John' in the church funeral service as John's *anam chara*: I can assure the world that John fulfilled his purpose.

The sadness and the loneliness of not having my love, my friend, my co-parent, my gardener, my business partner, my holiday buddy, is overbearing by times. To lose all so suddenly leaves a very sad and lonely space in my heart.

And it gets you when you least expect it – a thought, word, anything, nothing – just brings this ocean of grief that encapsulates you by times. I have learned to just go with it, to take the time to cry, to be sad and to feel the pain of that isolation.

Yet John is very present in my life and in our family in many ways. He just doesn't do the physical bits anymore – like bringing out the bins or pottering in the garden. We talk, I run things over with him – my sad times, my happy times – business, home, life – he knows them all. At Christmas, I recall saying to the girls: 'I didn't think he was going to do a *PS I Love You* on me.' It seems he leaves little messages around for me and the girls too. *'PS I Love You'* is the name of a lovely book, written by a very talented young Irish author, Cecelia Ahern, which I read on holidays a few years ago.

My dear mother had a lovely phrase that makes good sense to me now more than ever. It is: 'There's nothing wrong with a good cry, so long as you get up and go on afterwards.' Thank you Mam, for your wisdom. I have been reminded of that phrase quite a bit in this painful grieving journey.

The lesson I have learned from the parting of my life partner is that life is very short even if you do live to be 100. Seek inner spiritual direction and live your life from the inside out with honesty, integrity and truth as your core values, and clarity of your purpose in life as your mission, so that you live with passion and fulfilment as you fight the good fight to complete your journey of life.

If you want to live life – you had better start living your life right now. You are responsible for fulfilling your purpose and creating your legacy. Live your life now, and live it with purpose and be passionate by doing what is true to you. Live your life now with love in your heart and hope in your actions and trust in your creator that one day we will all meet again.

Florrie My Soul Mate Will Always Be Here

I never thought Florrie would die first. I always thought I would go first as I was a little older, but it was not to be. God's way is not our way. But let's go back to the beginning.

I met Florrie first when she was 15. We were both children of Newsagents. Her father had one of the oldest newsagents in Dublin, 'Lucky Duffy's, on Parnell Street. My father had died when I was ten and it happened my mother took over the business and ran it very successfully, as well as rearing her eight children. My father was 51 when he died. Although seven years younger than him, my mother lived until she was 87. Florrie's father, Paddy Duffy, was President of the Irish Newsagents Association, a post which my father had held many years before, although they never met.

One day I was visiting Paddy Duffy in his shop on newsagent's business and Florrie was there. I asked her would she come and work with us in our shop in Fairview, which she did. We started going out with each other when Florrie was 18, and then started a life-long romance that lasted until the day she died.

Florrie loved dancing so at every opportunity we'd 'trip the light fantastic' at all the ballrooms in Dublin. I was probably the worst dancer ever – talk about two left feet! But she put up with me. We also loved the movies and had regular seats each Sunday night at the Carlton Cinema in O'Connell Street. That meant they kept the same two seats for us every Sunday night once you collected the tickets by Thursday. So, you usually had the same people sitting each side of you every week. It seems odd now but then it was the norm.

After two years we got engaged and after three, when Florrie was 21, we got married. It was probably the happiest day of my life, marrying the girl of my dreams and when, 12 months later, our first baby, Gerard, was born, our joy was complete. We had four more children – Orla, David, Gráinne and Sinéad – and life

17

couldn't have been better. We had the usual dramas that every family has, children getting sick and so on but nothing serious. We were undoubtedly a very happy family and Florrie and myself never had a row. People find this hard to believe but it's true. We would have some differences of opinion, mostly about singers and records, but never a real row, so ours was a very happy home and Florrie liked nothing better than having the home full of the children's friends, running children's parties and always joining in the fun herself.

She loved shopping and always had the children turned out well. Indeed she bought all my clothes and those Hawaiian shirts I used to wear were all Florrie's idea. Every day was a happy day, apart from the usual flus and colds. Florrie was never sick. Her only visits to hospital were for the births of our five children, so you can imagine the shock when she was diagnosed with breast cancer.

I was on an outside broadcast doing my radio show from Waterford. Florrie came with me. While there she found a lump and when we got back to Dublin she immediately went to the doctor who sent her to get a breast check. A few days later she had to go to St Vincent's in Dublin for the result. I went with her. I'll never forget that room. There were about 40 women of all ages waiting for results. We had waited over an hour and Florrie's name hadn't been called up and I had a broadcast that day in the Virgin Megastore in Central Dublin for the launch of Joe Dolan's latest album, so I had to leave Florrie. My daughter Gráinne stayed with her. I went ahead with my radio show in Virgin Megastore and when the one o'clock news was on I phoned Gráinne and she told me Florrie had been diagnosed with breast cancer.

It was like being hit with a tram when I heard the news. I was halfway through my radio show and a few minutes later I had to do an interview with Joe Dolan. I know I did it but I can't remember what I asked him. To this day it's like a blur to me.

I couldn't believe how strong Florrie was. She had a mastectomy and after a course of chemo, it seemed to have cleared up. She went for check-ups every few months and every time she got the all clear until three years later when tragedy struck. She had gone for her usual check-up and they asked her to come back again for another check-up. We were packed and ready to go on holidays when she got the news that the cancer had returned. I was with her when she was told that there was a new treatment they were trying out. Florrie asked what would happen if she didn't have it. 'You'd be dead in six months', she was told, so they tried out a few new treatments that were working on some people, but none of them worked with Florrie. More tragedy was to come.

I used to go for a walk each morning in Bushy Park in Terenure and I began to get little tickles in my chest. The doctor sent me for a stress test but they said it was positive. I was still getting the feelings in my chest and my GP said I should get an angiogram. I wasn't going to go but Florrie insisted and they found my main artery was 95% blocked so I had to go in for a heart by-pass.

By this time Florrie was back in Vincent's and I was in Blackrock Clinic so both of us were in hospital at the same time. My operation was on 13 December so I had to spend Christmas in hospital. Our last Christmas together was in Blackrock Clinic where Florrie came to visit me so we could have a Christmas dinner together in a hospital room. I got out of hospital just after Christmas and Florrie died on 20 January. I'll always remember that last day. My son-in-law Rory drove me to Vincent's to see her and her only thoughts were of me. 'Would you go home and rest?' were the last words she spoke to me, even though weak, her dying words were thinking of me. Selfless to the last.

Even though I knew she was very ill, I didn't think she was going to die. I always thought that somehow she was going to get better. But I was only home from that last visit when my daughters Orla and Gráinne phoned me to tell me to come back as Florrie had gone into a coma. The whole family was with her when she died. She was sleeping and gently stopped breathing.

Florrie was my soul mate and I still talk to her every day. I miss her so much. When something happens at work I say to myself 'I must tell Florrie that', and then I remember, she's not there anymore.

They say time heals all wounds, but not for me. You never stop missing your loved one, but you do get better at dealing with it. I still feel her presence around the house – I believe her spirit is still here and that she watches over me and the family.

I would advise anyone grieving to talk to their loved one because I can't believe that when a person dies, that's it, there's nothing more. Their spirit must be still around and for me Florrie will always be here.

A Broken Open-Heart

Ciaran was a wonderful man, a beautiful man with rich black hair and an electric smile. He had a lust for life and adored people. He always considered himself to be a 'lucky' person. He was gentle and caring, interested in everybody he met. He reached out to people and could make a connection with a stranger in an instant. He was a true gentleman. We had met in our early twenties in London and were inseparable. Five years ago Ciaran died from cancer at the age of thirty one.

Our difficult journey began in April 2005 in Bristol where Ciaran and I lived. Ciaran was working hard as a social worker for the Sensory Services team, a job he thoroughly enjoyed, working with deaf/blind adults. He was an outstanding and skilled communicator and could make anybody feel at ease, young or old, from any background.

Ciaran had been feeling unwell for a few months and eventually went along to the GP. Within a month Ciaran was diagnosed with a terminal cancer and given weeks and months to live. We had been married less than a year.

Our lives stopped, our dreams shattered. The news came to us like an earth quake. No solid ground to stand on; no place of safety; hysteria and fear everywhere. But in time with good counsel and support from friends, family and professionals, the tremors eased and we found our feet again.

Ciaran underwent palliative chemotherapy in Bristol. However, this was unsuccessful and we were told the disease had spread. There was nothing more the doctors could do. At the first available opportunity we flew to Dublin (Ciaran's home) to see friends and family. It was at this time that Ciaran's condition worsened and he required emergency surgery. Soon after this Ciaran decided that Ireland was where he wanted to be, where he wanted to spend the rest of his days. So we packed up our belongings and moved to Dublin to be near his family.

In August 2005 Ciaran was referred to the local hospice.

Initially the word 'hospice' didn't fit into our vocabulary. It was an alien and frightening term. We wanted to hear the words 'hospital', 'treatment', 'remission' even 'cure', we wanted 'hope'. We soon learned however that 'hope' came in different forms so instead of hoping for a cure we hoped for longevity, we hoped for time, a sunny day, a pain-free day; we hoped to have a nice meal or watch a good movie. In essence we learned to live for the day.

In a very short time strong relationships were formed with the hospice team. We laughed and cried together. We made decisions together.

Ciaran always 'lived strong'. He never gave up hope. The cancer may have slowly devoured his body but his spirit continued to shine even brighter. Never once was he ever self-pitying or angry, just very sad that this terrible disease had latched onto his young body. Like a young boy playing out on the street being called in for his dinner, Ciaran didn't want to leave the fun but death was calling him in. He gave us as much as he could, he made us feel included and loved and he made us laugh, lots and lots.

Ciaran died at home in my arms in the early hours of a Sunday morning, April 2006. He had managed to live through twelve months. I do not know who or what stopped the fight. Ciaran, the cancer, my prayers? But it was time to stop. The referee was ringing the boxing bell for the next round but we didn't get up. We lay still, side by side in the deathly silence of the night. Momentarily my sorrow turned to anger and I cursed the cancer inside his body but this passed. Once I calmed myself I took comfort by caressing his curly black hair until I eventually fell asleep.

Like our cherished loved ones who have gone before us our grief is unique. Some writers describe a cycle or stages, but my personal experience has not been so structured or ordered but instead rather unruly, even frenzied at times.

Numbness, yearning, disorganisation, despair and depression are certainly all feelings I have felt at some point over the last five years but not necessarily in that order.

For me my grief has and continues to be like a bag of heavy

rocks I carry on my back. Some days I am energised and healthy and I can carry the load. I do feel the weight of my grief on my back pushing against me but I am strong and can manage.

Other days it can consume me. I can hardly stand up with the unrelenting weight of it all, the onerous tiredness at the knowledge that there is in fact no port to offload this burdensome cargo. I know I will always continue to carry the grief but that's OK. It's now part of who I am and who I will continue to be.

My own sense is that grief should always be treated with respect and never neglected. It should be tended and minded like a precious rose bush, pruned of its dead wood in order to encourage new growth and bloom so that its future, my future, can be shaped.

Like the rose, grief also has a beauty as it directly connects you to your love for your loved one, even though the thorns can sometimes cut deep.

So what has helped? I have wonderful friends and family who have walked alongside me on this difficult journey. Friends that have witnessed my struggles but not judged me or tried to direct me.

I have also always tried to maintain a connection with the outside world and even on the bleakest of days would take a walk or a drive, maybe go for a coffee. The healing touch from a gentle massage has regularly brought me to tears – tears that you didn't know were ready to fall. Exercise has also played a key role in helping me through difficult times – there is something very cathartic about jumping into a relaxing pool and submerging yourself in the warmth of the water. Like an unborn baby in the womb it offers a sense of protection and that feeling of being 'held'. It has also helped to combat the unyielding tiredness that accompanies grief.

As you have read, I have found it helpful to conceptualise my grief in many ways that has presented me with a language with which to describe my innermost thoughts and feelings. For my young nephews and niece, a memory box containing special personal items belonging to Ciaran provided an opportunity for them to sit and be close to him. They would perhaps smell a bottle of his aftershave, watch a funny home movie, tell one of his jokes, maybe put on one of his ties. There would always be tears and laughter and sometimes some difficult questions but it always felt a very healthy and safe means of helping them feel the pain and embark on their own journey of accepting the reality of their loss.

At the time of Ciaran's death, grief consumed me and it was very difficult to manage day to day. I felt a significant adjustment in all manner of ways as I faced my future alone, stripped of my identity. I was now widow not wife; Ms not Mrs, yet still a young woman just starting out in life. But as time passes I have found that my life has become bigger. My pain and grief remain the same size but the world around me has grown and continues to grow. I remember how lucky I have been to have found love and believe I have learnt some difficult but invaluable lessons at a relatively young age – lessons that will stay with me and which have given me an insight others my age might not have been afforded. I see these lessons as gifts.

I like Walters' (Walters, T. [1996] *A New Model of Grief: Bereavement and Biography*) take on grief, that is to say the purpose of grief is not to move on without those who have died but to find a secure place for them.

That secure place for me has been to continue to reminisce with friends and family about Ciaran and the legacy he has left.

In November 2007 Bristol City Council named a specialist centre after him in honour of the work he did. It was very comforting for us to be all together at the opening ceremony, celebrating such an extraordinary life in such an extraordinary way.

A football match is also played each year between friends in England and Ireland. The beauty of this tribute is that it gives us the opportunity to remember and memorialise Ciaran whilst playing the game he was so passionate about. It also gives us a day to come together, family and friends alike, to talk about the man that was so special to us.

But it's not just about looking back and remembering. It's about looking forward. In his short life, Ciaran always did have a unique way of bringing people together and he continues to do so.

I myself now volunteer at the hospice where Ciaran received such wonderful care. My role may be a simple one, making tea and coffee for patients, but the rewards are limitless. Whatever my frame of mind walking into the hospice, I always leave with the same feeling – that I am lucky, that life is precious and health can never be taken for granted. I regain lost perspective and focus that enables me to just let go of personal worries and re-member what is truly important.

So as my journey through bereavement continues I feel myself withdrawing my energy from my stolen future with Ciaran, choosing instead to reinvest it in new relationships. My heart may be broken but it is a broken heart that marks the beginning of a real love affair with the world. Not a conventional affair but a tarnished one, full of flaws and cracks. But with all it's mottled imperfections it is a broken-hearted, fearless love that can be of real help to us and others in pain.

For a person in grief, to hope under the most extreme of cir-cumstances is an act of defiance that permits that person to live their life on their own terms. It is part of human spirit to endure and give the future a chance to happen.

'To live with a broken open-heart is to experience life's full strength.'

Happy Memories of the Many Good Times

I first met Betty Carabini in 1965, when she was just sixteen years old. At the time, I was a young, successful showband musician, rather immodestly sporting a shiny flash car with several shiny, flashy suits to match.

On nights when we weren't playing, I frequented the No. 5 Club on Harcourt St., where the fare on offer was simple enough: rock & roll music, dancing, fizzy orange, crisps and most important of all, pretty girls!

It was on one of my first visits that I spotted a vivacious young woman who was not only a brilliant dancer, but also a 'dedicated follower of fashion'. Her clothes were inspired by the latest creations from swinging London's Carnaby St, her blonde hair close cropped like Jean Seberg's, and her eyes suitably sooted up like Dusty Springfield. I was smitten!

Hopelessly deficient in the terpsichorean arts as I was, it took me ages to pluck up the courage to ask her to dance, and I was both surprised and delighted when she accepted me as a dancing partner. This quickly led to visits to the cinema and a few jars in the pub. This continued until Betty's eighteenth birthday loomed, and thoughts turned to the consideration of marriage. I remember asking her what she thought of our prospects. She replied, 'Look, we'll plan for six months, anything beyond that will be a bonus!' The bonus was over forty years!

Betty was a working-class girl who, after her father's early death, decided to leave school at fourteen, get a job and in that way try to help her struggling family. Yet despite this lack of formal education, she was confident and at ease in all situations, formal or otherwise. Similarly, she was my most important critic, and often the only one I'd listen to. I cannot think of a single picture of mine which wasn't improved by comments from Betty after viewing it as a work in progress.

Betty was not only the inspiration for, but also the subject of, some of my more important pictures. As well as being a great support to me throughout my career as an artist, she was also, and here I quote a colleague,'a great friend to all Irish artists'. In 1981, the first mutual support organisation for Irish artists was established, the Association of Artists in Ireland, and Betty was appointed as its first administrator. After this, she and her friend, artist Jacqueline Stanley, established the National Portrait Exhibition.

In 1986, Betty had a terrible accident, which resulted in a serious brain injury. I remember her neurologist saying to me, 'a brain injury is not like a broken arm, it's far more complicated than that.' As it turned out, Betty, her family and her friends had to cope with the fallout from that unfortunate accident for the rest of her life.

Betty's last few years were blighted with ill health, but even her darkest days were brightened by the presence of her grandchildren, Ava and Ethan. She indulged them at every opportunity. Once, when I cautioned her about this tendency of hers, she replied with a withering look, 'What role is there for grandparents other than to spoil their grandchildren?'

I suppose it is only to be expected, after a lifetime together, that given her sudden passing, I would have a massive Betty-shaped void at the centre of my life. What I have found surprising, however, is that there seems to be a portion of me missing as well, that part that went to form the couple we once were.

Having lost both my parents many years ago, I am well aware of the healing qualities of time. Nevertheless, I firmly believe that I will always retain a certain inexplicable sense of emptiness at my core.

There can be no doubt that nature helps us get through these hugely traumatic experiences. For example, I find that when I think of Betty, my memory banks swell with happy memories of the many good times we had together, while at the same time, amazingly, recollections of dark and difficult experiences seem to sink to the bottom and become almost impossible to retrieve.

As the process continues, I trust that sometime in the future when thoughts of Betty begin to surface that, instead of being tinged with pain and sadness, they will be bathed in a warm glow of happy recollections of a long life together.

27

Learning to Live in a New Way

'Say goodbye to the world you thought you lived in' played on the radio and that summed up how I felt.

I could not turn off the life I led for twenty-five years as a wife; how could I function without the man I had grown along side for over thirty years? It is the only life I knew. I had forgotten how to be a single person. I was half a couple and inside I was half a person and I had no idea what to do next.

Death came swiftly. An operation to remove a small contained tumour went wrong and septic shock took hold. Sitting in the intensive care unit, a timeless place, where every bleep can hail potential recovery or disaster, I prayed and made promises, bartered some of my life for a few more years shared with this man who now hovered between life and death. His body, bloated beyond recognition, was wired like a puppet to his new master, a life support machine. The pledges went unnoticed as at 13.31 p.m. on 13 July death won, the machine ended its shift, and I was a widow.

Widow – how I hated that word. Empty, bereft, relict of another, thrown into the twilight zone of life. I Google searched it and Google suggested that perhaps I intended to search for windows. I mused, I was shattered but I was more interested in doors really. Instructions on how to close the door on a really lovely life with a truly good man and maybe one day open a new one to a future free from the pain of widowhood.

I had no map for this new journey, no *Lonely Planet* guidebook. My guide, my comforter, my lover, my friend, the person I needed most was gone from me and I was shocked to numbness.

We had a lovely funeral, such a crazy way to describe a funeral, but it was the perfect funeral for the perfect farmer. It was held in wonderful sunshine on a golden harvest day. The folk group sang, the birds sang, the corn crackled, the air smelt sweet with lilies. Rough farm hands shook trembling ones. Strong men had tears in their eyes. I had retreated to my cocoon. Shock stuns to protect. I viewed myself from a parallel place but I remember, we had a lovely funeral.

Being surrounded by people cushioned the reality for a while. Visitors called bearing gifts, flowers, scones, apple tarts, a book, company that filled the emptiness. But after six weeks the torrent of visitors dried up and solitude filled the space. Loneliness showed its white face. Pain set in, grief had arrived. I reacted, I ducked and dived to avoid grief, but it followed me. It stopped me eating, it stopped me sleeping, it altered my thinking, and it inflicted a brain injury. It brought its friend 'fear' to hunt me down and keep me cornered. There was no way to escape grief. Sleep allowed me to hide for a few hours but it was never long enough. My first waking thought was 'Oh no, I am alive and I am a widow.' My husband's last words were, 'I don't think I will get through this', and I started to think that too.

There was no pleasure in life anymore. I existed. My weight dropped, I didn't miss it. It was my most successful diet – the Death Watchers Plan. Two stone vanished in three months. From a health point of view I felt energetic, and I apparently looked well as people started to comment and congratulate me on my new slim appearance. The compliments almost offended me especially when they wanted to know my secret formulae. I had also started to wear make-up. It was a necessary cover-up. Going to the shops for milk with a scalded face would have brought unwelcome attention, so I applied green cover stick to the red face and then plastered over that with foundation. I never wore much make-up so I had spent thirty years looking pretty unnoticeable. Make-up is powerful stuff.

One day, someone stopped me and asked me how I was. I was bluntly honest and replied that I existed somewhere close to hell. My enquirer was visibly taken aback and I knew I had made my first mistake. I needed people to greet me on the street without the fear of what I might land on them so I learned my first lesson – people who ask how you are, are seldom ready for the real answer. To say I was fine, might have been easier but I could not stomach that, so my new expression 'learning to live in a new way' was the best I would come up with.

My second lesson was not to decline invitations. I did not want to run the risk of being abandoned. In the beginning I made myself go out and usually had an escape plan if I felt overpowered by sadness or bitterness. I felt pretty hard done by but I never shared that in public. In time I discovered that I was a sociable person and I needed people. Out of necessity I also learned to be alone and to be my own best friend.

For me grief was like labour. It was giving birth to a new way of living. The pain came in waves, grip releasing just when I felt I could not take much more. The pain remained just about bearable. Time did not heal but time brought an evolution of new ways to cope. Holding on to the past continues until destiny creates an acceptable alternative and I feel that is where grief differs between individuals.

Help came in many ways. I found too many co-incidences to dismiss as mere chance happenings. It helped me to believe that in grief we are given enough help to get us through. Grief is a natural process and therefore our bodies are built to handle it. That does not belittle its power. Grief was and continues to be my most powerful life experience. It alters the person it enters and leaves on its own terms and in its own time frame. Its capacity to ambush is amazing and our ability to withstand it and grow is empowering. We each experience it as amateurs and become experts.

More words of that song swell up in me:

> Smile like you mean it, and let yourself let go ...
> say goodbye to the world you thought you lived in.
> Take a bow, play the part of a lonely, lonely heart,
> say goodbye to the world you thought you lived in.
> I never, never, forget my story, my face is not sad,
> but inside I am sad.

Bernie O'Reilly – widowed 5 years in July 2011. I was 49 when my fifty-year-old fit husband died. I have one daughter who is 23 now.

(The lyrics are from Mika – *Any Other World* – from the CD *Life in Cartoon Motion* – I do not have his permission to use his words, but I wrote them in my head before he started singing them to me but he owns the copyright.)

STORY WRITTEN BY JIM REDMOND (PARTNER) & ALICE (DAUGHTER)

Treasured Memories of Lou

Lucy (known as Lou) died on the 27 August 2009, 2 days before her eighty-second birthday from pneumonia associated with complications from inclusion body myopathy.

Lou was a born extrovert, a classic beauty, passionate, full of life and energy. She was involved in everything (drama, social work, charities and the GAA), you name it she was associated with it at some stage. She loved to walk and be out and about, she had a great sense of humour and fun. Lou was a fighter and was always one. Through her life she fought to have the best for her children, she worked tirelessly for charities and organisations (St Vincent De Paul, Community Information Centre, Lions Club, GAA, Mental Health Association, Wicklow County Mental Hospital in Ashford). She embraced things with a great passion; there were no half measures. Little did we know that this fighting spirit would be needed to carry her through years of ill health.

From about 2000, Lou started to have mobility issues and she had repeated falling episodes and whilst lucky never to break bones, she experienced difficulties walking and getting in and out of the car, bed and chairs. In time, Lou developed swallow problems and she found it increasingly difficult to eat and keep food down. Physically she looked frail having lost a lot of weight and muscle mass. During this time frame no stone was left unturned to find the root cause of her illness; with a trail beaten to numerous specialists. However, there were no answers, only a growing list of medical issues (including glaucoma, high blood-pressure, mini-strokes and Parkinsons) which resulted in her taking an ever increasing amount of medication.

Let me fast forward to 2006/7 when Lou's health had deteriorated to such an extent that we were afraid to leave her by herself even for short periods of time. I must point out that Lou's medical issues were just physical. She remained sharp, witty, humorous and alert and she only experienced loss of mental status for very short episodes near the end of her life.

Lou's final acceptance of her disease came at a point in time when her swallow was gone so bad that she could not eat. Following two extended stays in St Vincent's hospital with its fantastic care, her disease was eventually diagnosed as inclusion body myopathy. Most of her associated ailments were related to the disease. Whist this was a relief, there were two overwhelming reactions – her disease could be hereditary, and we were worried for our families, and what was the road ahead. The predicted road ahead was of further deterioration in muscle mass which would eventually lead to respiratory failure.

Her overriding message and consistent plea was she wanted to go home to her family, her house, her rose garden and the smell of the sea. During her long stays in hospital a steady supply of roses, spray bottles of sea water, sand and shells were by her bedside to help her close her eyes and experience the smell of home.

We promised we would get her home and keep her home but she needed to get herself well enough to do so. We had multiple set backs in this process including repeated bouts of pneumonia, MRSA, etc. Lou earned the name of 'Lucy Lazarus' in hospital for her numerous death bed recoveries. Once after coming out of a serious episode the doctor and nurses were trying to get a response from Lou – they repeatedly asked her 'What's your name?' She forced out a response and it was 'Lazarus'. The medical team thought she was not 'with it at all'. My sister and I were there and despite the seriousness of the situation we could not stop laughing, this to me epitomised Lou's sense of fun, humour and spirit.

Lou came home like the queen to cut the ribbon on the way in the door. We made the decision to make an event of it and she deserved it. She was determined to get well enough to go home and she did. After her last long stay in hospital Lucy got home two days before her eightieth birthday; we had a party planned but in true Lucy form she was determined it would not be cancelled. Once home the worry became 'I need to get a few bits done (hair, nails, facial)' and 'What will I wear?'

The next sixteen months was a busy but happy time. It became a haze of routine, dispersed with bouts of pneumonia. Yet, that said Lucy was happy in herself. She got out for drives when possible, she enjoyed her family and the company of her 'team' of carers. When she could she took a few steps aided with two people and she had an exercise bike that she could sit in her chair and pedal away. This gave her some much needed exercise to help muscle tone and lung function.

The decision had been made: she would not return to hospital and given the nature of the disease, we all knew that one serious flu would take her away from us. In true Lucy form, the Friday before she died she woke with the resolve she wanted to go shopping and despite the fact she was not in great shape, she would not take no for an answer. We headed to our local shopping centre and had a serious amount of fun, she bought loads of gifts for all. I think she knew it was her last *Hurrah*.

She met some of her buddies – this to me is a treasured memory and epitomised my Mum when she announced to me 'get your father to go an' have a coffee so we can spend some money! Lou's death came quicker than expected in the end. She just slipped away without saying goodbye while we were saying the rosary.

Lessons learnt for me are numerous. Superhuman efforts can be made but there has to be a balance between your life, your work, the support of the main carer and the care of an ill parent. Progressive disease is debilitating, slow and painful, as in Lucy's case it lasted for more than ten years. It's like a marathon, you have to pace yourself, but unlike a marathon you don't know when you will reach the finishing line.

My message to you is that you may not be able to do everything you want but you need to make sure that what you do matters. There is a balancing act between fulfilling your need as a person in visiting an ill parent out of obligation and acting as a support mechanism to the ill parent and main carer. A change in the norm and routine is probably the biggest gift a visiting sibling, friend or family member brings. This acts as a great distraction, a different topic for conversation and much needed rest time for the main carer.

From my perspective, dignity and fun are the most important things for a person who is suffering from a progressive illness.

They are human beings with feelings, needs and fears. They deserve to be treated with dignity and still have a bit of fun in their life. They need to be able to adapt to their illness and still retain some of the things they enjoy. Lou always loved reading; when her sight became too bad to read, she re-discovered her love of radio and she switched from reading to listening to novels on CD. Lou wasn't supposed to eat or drink but every so often she had to have a taste of tea, a lick of ice-cream or a small piece of chocolate. Illness is serious and all consuming but even if it means breaking the rules every now and then, this is needed to feel human. Lou's disease cut her off from her social outlets, her freedom, her friends and hobbies. This to her, I think, was worse than her disease.

How do we feel now 18 months on?
We feel humbled by Lou: the way she accepted her illness, her appreciation and her joy at being at home, her pride in her appearance, her love and dependence on Dad, her fight and her stubborn resolve not to give up.

Jim is content, healthy, full of pride for his family and their achievements and immensely proud of the way they helped to mind their Mum. Jim still goes up to visit Lou's grave most days and speaks about her as if she is still alive. He is doing well but lonely after fifty-two years of marriage. He has embraced a new life: walking, golf, visiting family and bridge – the gap of losing Lou will never be filled but he is getting on with life and enjoying this different existence.

How do the rest of us feel? We know it was Lou's time but we miss her wicked sense of humour and her sense of fun. The house is different now, you walk in and still expect to see her in her chair waiting to have a chat. The stoic way she approached life and her disease is a lesson to us all. She had an indeterminable bond with her grandkids. We see her traits, her beautiful blue eyes and her sense of fun in them every day. Nana Lou may have left us physically but her presence lives on in them forever.

Lou's rose garden remains like a memorial to her, her beauty, her fifty-two years of marriage to Jim and a perfection we should all strive for.

Things Seem Better in the Light

Just another family holiday! Myself, Chris (my husband) and our two children, Andrew aged sixteen and Laura aged fourteen, were staying in Lanzarote, and it was here that the nightmare began. One evening Chris told me that he had been having problems passing urine. He had been having symptoms for nearly three months, with urgency and not passing much urine. I had worked in the Urology Department as a Medical Secretary and knew that this could be serious in some cases but, as Chris was only fifty-five, I thought it was probably an infection or something like that. It took Chris another two months, with constant nagging, to go and see our GP who did some blood tests. When we went for the results, he told us Chris had a raised Prostate specific antigen (PSA) and also raised lymphocytes in his blood.

We booked two appointments, one for the urologist about his PSA and the other for the haematologist about his blood. The urologist advised him to have a biopsy and when I went to collect him afterwards the nurse just said, 'You do know it's prostate cancer.' This was the first time we had heard this and both of us were in shock. Nevertheless Chris wanted to go out for a meal that night and I can only think he wanted things to be as normal as possible, even though I found every mouthful hard to swallow. That night we got into bed and turned the lights out and I just cried. I turned the *en suite* light on as I knew that if I had a light on I would not cry as Chris would be able to see me. And from that moment on Chris never saw me cry again and to this day I still sleep with the light on as darkness makes me remember how utterly devastated I felt that day and things always seem so much better in the light.

Chris was put on hormone tablets in an effort to reduce his PSA and that same month he went to the haematologist who told Chris that not only did he have prostate cancer but that he had chronic lymphocytic leukaemia as well. Both these conditions are more prevalent in older patients so though Chris had never

35

looked his age, he had the body (apparently) of someone a lot older and we used to joke about this – what else could we do? No treatment was given for the leukaemia as being chronic it was something that would go on for years.

We discussed who to tell about the diagnosis and prognosis of his condition. Chris wanted as few people as possible to know about this as he just wanted to live a normal life with nobody questioning how he was or looking at him strangely or talking about him or offering sympathy. He also did not want the children to know at that time as he wanted them to continue treating him as they had always done. We knew that if we said he had cancer, and told them the prognosis, it would have altered all of our lives.

When Chris first went back to the urologist after a blood test, his PSA had gone down and we were over the moon. He was advised to have radiotherapy as the cancer from the prostate would sometimes spread to organs nearby and this could help to stop this from happening. Chris underwent seven weeks of radiotherapy (Monday to Friday) up in London. He did not have a day off work, going into work in the morning, catching a tube to the hospital, having the radiotherapy and then going back to work. I still marvel that he did this, never complaining and being truly remarkable in the way he coped with everything that had been handed to him. Unfortunately, the tablets did not work and he was put on injections, which also did not work and his PSA kept rising meaning that the cancer was moving through his body.

Chris continued going to work and hardly told anyone there that he was ill except for a couple of close friends. He maintained that when people asked how he was, he just wanted it to be a general how was he rather than related to his illness and so felt that there was no need for people to know. He had hardly any time off work so nobody knew any different. People close to us were told but to look at him you would not have guessed he was ill and that this horrible illness was careering through his body at a rate of knots with nothing to prevent it. As I could not cry in front of Chris I used to spend days racked with grief on my own whilst he was at work, only putting on 'my face' and freshening up when he was due in, so that he never knew, as it would have upset him to know how I felt. That is how stoical he was, it should have been him racked with grief but he would have been worried about me.

I did eventually tell the children but not till the beginning of 2007 and then I just dropped into the conversation about their dad being ill, and having cancer and that everything was being done for him that could be done. I did not mention the possibility that he could die as Chris would not have wanted this.

In December 2007, Chris decided he would give up work due to ill health, even though he was still working every day. Someone came from his firm and discussed it all with us and it was nice to think that we would have some time together when we could do all the things we had wanted to – seeing *The Phantom of the Opera* in London, being one of the things. However, that same day Chris had an appointment at the Oncology Clinic and when he went there his haemoglobin was very low and they admitted him for a blood transfusion and he came out the next day. That night he tried to talk to me about him dying. I told him I did not want to talk about it. Rightly or wrongly admitting he might die was not something I wanted to do. On the Friday night I noticed that he was not going to the toilet and he seemed to be distant. He was also scratching himself a lot. With my limited medical knowledge, I knew his kidneys were obviously not working well. On the Saturday, he seemed better, but by the Sunday morning he was not himself. He went into the shower and scrubbed himself again and again and again. It took me ages to get him out of there. When I did get him out and he went to get dressed he put two T-shirts on, one on top of the other and one inside out. I therefore took him to the hospital and he was admitted.

Having spent most of the day at the hospital the medical team decided his kidneys were not functioning properly and wanted to do an operation to relieve this but would wait till the next day. I went home and got to bed at 1.30ish only to be woken at about 4 a.m. by the nurse telling me they were not going to do the operation and that he was very ill. I asked if I should come up and she just kept repeating that he was very ill. I had to get both the children up, phone his daughter, Melanie, from his first marriage and his sister and tell them all how ill he was. We all went up to the hospital and sat around the bed in turns. I am sure he must have thought it was strange all of us being there although in my heart I hope he did not realise why we were there. I then had to see the consultant and begged them to do the operation to relieve his kidneys. They agreed but a few hours later Chris had a fit and they decided against this again. I then argued that I wanted the operation and saw another consultant but nobody would back me up and I knew I could do no more. Andrew and Laura went home along with Melanie and I stayed with Heather, his sister.

Heather and myself stayed in the room with Chris, I was talking to him and holding his hand and willing him to squeeze my fingers. Unfortunately, when I asked him to let me know that he knew we were there, he did not respond. I have never felt so helpless. I watched Chris die on Tuesday 11 December 2007 at 7.00 p.m. He was peaceful but I cannot say that it was nice to be there with him. I know that I never want to watch anyone die again. I think I was in shock, I really cannot explain how I felt and it all seems a blur. I went into autopilot as I had to go and tell the nurse that he had just died, which seems absurd now. Then I had to phone my children to tell them their father had died and then I sent one text to loads of people to let them know what had happened.

Going home from the hospital was surreal as well. Leaving Chris alone was heart-wrenchingly awful. Heather begged the nurses before we left not to leave him as she could not bear to think of him being on his own. The taxi driver who took us home asked if we had had a nice day. Unfortunately, I told him the truth as I did not have the ability to make something up. I did not want to deny Chris and hopefully he will never ask that question again to someone coming out of a hospital. We arrived home and I just hugged our children.

The days after Chris died are a blur. We relished being together in our 'bubble' as we called it to get through each day. However, having brilliant family and friends made this whole journey easier. The children and myself never cried in front of each other, just something we did not do even at the funeral. From my point of view I felt that if they saw me upset then they would be upset and I think they thought this also.

If it had not been for our friend, Frances (a living Angel), who lived up the road I think we would have all starved as I had no sense of time and no ability to do anything. Plates of food arrived every day and she took us to all the appointments needed and even arranged the funeral for me – something I am eternally grateful for as I know I could not have done it myself. There were lots of friends and family who helped at the funeral and I can never thank them enough. The funeral went well but I remember thinking that Chris was not in the coffin. It was just a body and that he was still with us and that is how I got through the day and every day since.

The last three years have been difficult at times. The first year and all the anniversary dates were the most difficult. There are other anniversaries I have to get through as well. One evening after Chris was diagnosed he sat at the table with me over dinner and said he wanted to see Laura reach eighteen, Andrew reach twenty-one and wanted to be there for our twenty-fifth wedding anniversary. He did not manage any of these. For the first year at least I would find myself going to the cemetery every day or two. If I had a bad day I would go and stand by the grave and cry and berate Chris for leaving me alone to cope with everything. The children have been marvellous and we talk about Chris and have pictures around the house so that he is always in our thoughts. The children miss Chris in different ways. Andrew works in London and knows he would have been travelling to and from London and going to the pub with him, and Laura knows that he will not be there to walk her down the aisle when she marries. I am also sure she missed him when learning to drive as he had so much more patience than me. Myself, I have had lots of sleepless nights where I have thought there could be no water left to come out of my eyes but still the tears come. I miss having someone with me, someone to discuss the children with, someone to help me make decisions. You never know how much you truly miss and rely on someone until they are gone. The emptiness is all consuming and something I have had to come to terms with.

I have learnt through all this the value of relatives and friends. In all the darkness that enveloped us, there was always someone there who could help and guide us through. We have been truly blessed. Many decisions I made about Chris and his illness were open to criticism by some people but in my mind I did what was best for me and my family and I do think I made the right decisions. I know some people thought I should have told the children earlier but nothing would have been gained by it. Not all families are the same; you need to do what is best for your family and not what people tell you to do.

I have always felt that Chris is with us wherever we are, which is a great comfort to me. This might sound weird to some people but I know he would never ever leave us and although he had to bodily go, spiritually he has stayed with us. Whilst out driving once in the car not long after Chris died, I smelt his aftershave and I knew he was there with me. It did not frighten me and in fact I thought it was quite lovely and just reaffirmed my belief that he is still with us, caring and looking after us all. I am still angry with myself that I could not find a way to save him by reading any and every available article on prostate cancer. Life goes on, but memories help get us through. I am grateful for the years that we had together though sad for all that he has missed and will miss.

Finding a Place after Marge's Passing

Marge died at the age of forty-three as a result of multiple brain tumours and we only knew she was terminal for five days. The first shock came when the doctor took us into the hall and said: 'In cases like this, there is nothing we can do except make the patient comfortable.' The second shock came about a month after we buried her, with the realisation of just how alone I was.

Her siblings had another sibling; her parents had other children; my three, teenage children still had a parent; but I had lost my only wife, partner and best friend. At church, people filled in the roles she used to fill; and the same at the schools our children attended. But there was no one to do all the things she had done for me, and no one for me to do all the things I had done for her. It was like half of me left and there was nowhere to look to find it.

Actually, I lost even more. I lost my children to their immersion in friends and school activities. Plus Marge's and my life had revolved completely around the friendships we had with other couples and families at church and at school. For the first 30 days, we had more food and company than we could handle. Then nothing – no calls, no invitations, no company. No one had any idea about how to talk to me. No one wanted anything to do with a single man in a married world; and I didn't know any single people. At that moment all I had left was breathing, sleeping and eating; and food tasted like paste.

It was my first realisation about just how much we, and all the people with whom we had surrounded ourselves, had indulged in self-serving insulation from the real world. In fact, it was the beginning of an ongoing quest to understand just how much our human nature, the tendency to look after ourselves, dominates our human spirit, the tendency to consider the needs of others.

We had a lot of delegated tasks that each one of us took care of for our family; mine being mostly 'outside' tasks, such as earning a living, taking care of the yard, keeping the cars running, dealing with difficult people or situations. Hers were things like paying the bills, managing our social calendar, preparing meals, keeping the house nice, making sure everyone's clothes got washed. Then we shared things like transportation, coaching and community involvement.

The very first task I had was to take over responsibility for the cheque book. I found that the tumours had taken their toll in ways I could never have imagined. I couldn't even read the cheque register for about three pages back. So I had to start making calls, visiting the bank and, essentially, rebuilding our accounts. Then I had to try to reorganise all the records she had been maintaining for the various groups and projects we had been involved with and get them to the proper individuals.

At the same time, we had to try to sit down as a family and re-distribute the family workload. The first few times we tried it were disasters. As soon as one person started crying, one or more of us would lose their composure and everyone would head for their rooms. It literally took weeks before we had a smoothly running household again and it would have taken way longer if Marge hadn't taught our daughters a lot about cooking. Stuff like washing clothes were things we could read about and master over time. But cooking was an art and, like most good Italian mothers, she had shared that art with our daughters right from the beginning.

During those weeks, I didn't like it when I had to be alone for any length of time but, at the same time, I often needed to go off by myself so that no one would see me crying. It would just trigger someone else and the last thing we needed was an epidemic. So we moved through life somewhat like robots for a long time. It was not a life; it was barely an existence.

Marge had died in April and, by the following September, I was feeling so bad that I thought I must be dying too. And then, somehow, I just decided I had to have a life. If none of our old friends wanted anything to do with me and, if my children only wanted to be involved in activities with their teenage friends, then it was up to me to make a change. I didn't know where to start; I only knew I had no choice.

So I took stock. I knew I needed to be around people again. I knew I needed to find people who were experiencing similar circumstances to mine, so that I could talk with them and they would get it. And I knew I wasn't ready to try having a relationship. The last thing I needed was to be with just one person – I needed to be with groups. Right in the middle of that, someone at work told me about a group called Parents Without Partners. I will tell you right now that it could have been any one of numerous similar groups I have discovered since then.

This particular group had meetings with speakers. They had round-table discussions, they had social time at every meeting, and they even had parties once a month for something a little livelier. It sounded like a good possibility. I found a chapter, somewhat far from home, which met on a Tuesday night, a night on which I didn't have any obligations to my family. The place was easy enough to find but, when I got there, I discovered I didn't know what to do or how to be. I stood against the wall and just watched people arrive. Then I sat down when everyone else did and listened to a speaker about some innocuous subject that I can't even remember.

Finally, as the speaker finished, people got up and started talking to each other like normal people do and someone just came up to me and asked me how I was. It was that easy. Then I spoke with another person and another person and another person. We had some refreshments and there was ordinary conversation about upcoming speakers and topics and events and I just felt myself coming alive. I discovered that I wasn't alone, that life would go on, and that I could even smile again.

However, the lesson I learned is not just one to be shared with others who lose a spouse. It is one that should be known among those who haven't suffered that tragedy too. For those who have, they need to know that they still have a place in the world as soon as they are ready to go and search for it. For those who know them, the lesson is that that person still needs you and that they are the same person they were before. You don't have to be afraid of them. You don't have to avoid them. Just reach out with your hand and your ear and your smile. You are their hope.

43

Getting My Peace Back

After reading the story *'Grieving: a Beginners Guide'*, I realised I could relate to it, this was a terrible experience. On the Sunday morning after my husband Pat's death, I went to Mass in the local church. I was anxious about going because I know many people in the parish and I did not feel up to chatting to anyone and I was hoping no one would stop to talk to me.

When Mass was over and I returned home to my house I found my family were clearing out my husband's clothes and belongings. They thought it was a good time to sort out his belongings while I was away out of the house, but unfortunately they did not realise that at that time there was not going to be a right time for me to ever do this. I broke down and cried uncontrollably, I sobbed and said that is all I have left and would they please understand that I did not want anyone touching Pat's belongings and would they please leave them alone. They decided they would only get rid of the working clothes and leave the rest of Pat's belongings alone for the moment until I was able to deal with this.

After one year passed I felt that I was ready to go through Pat's clothes and belongings. So I phoned my friend and asked her would she mind helping me bring the clothes to the nearest charity shop. I had no regrets after the clothes were gone as I was happy that other people would make use of them.

Most days my friend rang me and asked if I'd like to go for a walk. I found this very helpful, she always knew the right thing to say and what not to say. I found this very comforting and reassuring and very important to me at my time of need. I noticed I became forgetful and not remembering where I put things was very upsetting to me. At times I thought I was going senile, but my friend assured me that was not happening. She told me she felt the same as if she was losing her mind when she lost her husband. 'Mind blanks' is what my friend called it, this information was very reassuring and gave me a great lift to know I was not losing my mind but I was normal like any grieving person.

The grief I was going through was not what I expected. Some days I'd be sad thinking of the good times we had together and how they can't ever happen again now he is no longer with me. Other days I would be angry with him for leaving me, asking him why he had to die? When a day like this came and panic set in there was only one thing to do. I would ask God to help me. After lots of crying I would get my peace back. I didn't think grieving could be so exhausting, I got so tired and drained after one of those days when all seemed lost.

I remember so well one day, many months after my husband died, I went with my sister to see a friend in hospital. It was the hospital where my husband was after he had taken ill. When I came to the ward he had been in I froze, then it all flooded back as if it had happened on that day.

My father died seven years before my husband. I thought it might have been a little easier, but it wasn't. In fact it was much harder to grieve for my husband: all the little things we shared together and when there were problems he was there to share them with me. Now he was no longer there to listen to me. I worked for a few hours three mornings a week. I returned to work five weeks after my husband's death. I decided it would be best for me. It would have been so easy to stay indoors and not go out so I could avoid meeting people.

My husband and I went to bingo a couple of nights each week, so when he died my friends and neighbours would ask me each week to go with them, but I could not bring myself to go. But after ten months I was ready to go back. I believe you can't go back to doing anything until you are ready, no matter how long it takes.

My daughter was always there for me. We can't always expect our families to give a lot of time as they have their own families.

I had always looked forward to my husband's retirement with the free pass to travel around Ireland to the places we never had a chance to visit. But my husband died three weeks prior to his retirement so that put an end to all my expectations.

There are good days and bad days while grieving, the good days are very good with the nice memories, the bad days are birthdays, anniversaries, Easter and Christmas time. I was blessed because my family were always there at those special times.

If days went by and I did not remember to grieve I thought it was very wrong but I learned as time went by that it was good, it was a letting go which is not a bad thing.

Having flashbacks of my husband's death was not unusual. It perhaps helped me in a lot of ways to get through my grieving or perhaps lessens the pain.

CHAPTER TWO

Parents' Stories

The death of a child is the single most traumatic event in medicine. To lose a child is to lose a piece of yourself
Dr Burton Grebin

There is no greater unconditional love than the love of a parent for their child. When that love cycle is broken through the death of your child, the pain is severe, the loss is permanent, the future is unbearable and the healing process takes forever.

There are no shortcuts through the grieving process as you battle through the many emotions and many variations of the different emotions. Yet in these times of brokenness, you dig deep for strength and grace to somehow fill the space and keep you alive.

As we grapple with life anew, knowing there is no such thing as 'forever' ever again.

The irony in death is that there is life and life takes on a different complexion as we strive to grow and live again.

The following stories of life and love and death and suffering and grieving are spoken from the heart of each parent. We hope you receive peace, hope and consolation in the passages of stories told by parents whose children have died.

Cherry Blossom Petal

Our daughter Sinead was born on 16 August 1987 at about 3.00 a.m. Earlier my husband Donal and I had set off eagerly from Arklow to travel to The National Maternity Hospital, Holles St, Dublin. We had only travelled half way when I realised that this baby was not going to wait much longer to make an appearance. We pulled over, hubby rang for an ambulance, thankfully it arrived promptly, and a few minutes later our Sinead had arrived. Always a girl who liked a dramatic entrance.

Oh! What a feeling arriving at the Maternity Hospital with your baby already in our arms. She was beautiful with a head of dark hair. Everyone said she would lose that hair, but no! It grew thick and curly. She was the apple of her dad's eye, and she had him wrapped around her little finger from that first moment, and she knew it. Her brother David was just a year old. He soon became very protective of his little sister; he checked everyone out before he let them get too near. Eighteen months later Thomas joined our little family, a little blonde baby with the deepest of dimples. Our home was filled with the noise of children playing, crying, laughing, arguing, and an air of general mayhem reigned.

Three children under three, yikes! How Sinead bossed those two brothers of hers around. She was bright, bubbly, and never stuck for a word. Her ambition as a little girl was to go to college, and then to work in Marks and Spencers. She was the spokesperson of the group, and yes, her brothers were right: she was a little bossy boots at times, although she could also be extremely sensitive sometimes.

Eight years later Eimear, our second daughter, was born to complete our family. Sinead was so excited, and they all adored their new little sister. Poor Donal was once again putty in a little girl's hand. We felt so blessed, so lucky, and never took our good fortune for granted. I relished my role as stay at home mammy. I loved sharing the everyday ups and downs of childhood with my little gang. Drop-offs for schools, sleepovers, swimming, tennis, football, not to mention karate and tae kwon do were all part of the weekly routine. Thomas and Sinead were strong swimmers and loved to swim together. I remember one of those lovely autumn days having the whole beach to ourselves at Brittas Bay and looking around seeing them both too far out, heads bobbing about amongst the white horses, and their dad frantically waving his arms to get them back ashore. I remember a million things.

Ironically, I started working outside the home four weeks before Sinead's death, something that was to haunt me for a very long time to come. Three weeks into the new job, as I was heading out to work, Sinead slipped a little note into my hand to say she was feeling down in herself, and she didn't know why. It stopped me in my tracks. I brought her to our GP, and although she felt Sinead was okay she decided to try her on an anti-depressant to help her over this low spell. I believed they would work, and she would soon feel much better, which for most people is the positive outcome. Sinead had never been depressed before so I felt in no time she would turn a corner. Over the next few days I tried to reassure her by telling her we loved her, and that soon she would feel much better. Tragically this was not how Sinead's story unfolded.

It was 3 May 2004, a Bank Holiday Monday. A lovely sunny day, before I left for work that morning, I looked in on Sinead. She was asleep, and looked so peaceful, I didn't want to disturb her, so I left for work without saying goodbye.

We have a beautiful, very large cherry blossom tree in our garden which only blooms for a very short time. As I was heading out to work that morning I looked at the blossoms beginning to appear, and I thought, now that's a sure sign summer is on it's way.

Later on in work, at about three o' clock, something caught my eye. I looked up, and saw Donal in the distance. As he came closer I smiled … he didn't smile back. He looked ashen. My mind started racing. What was going on? Then I noticed there was a policeman with him, and I knew: Oh God! Oh God!

49

Everything started slowing down. They were walking towards me ... I wanted to run ... I couldn't bear to hear what they were going to say, but my legs had stopped working. They were speaking now telling me Sinead had taken her own life. She was dead. I heard screaming. The World was moving in slow motion. I don't know how they got me to the car to bring me home, but I do remember thinking, this was all a horrible mistake. I would see Sinead, and I would make everything okay. She might still be alive, but there were to be no miracles that day.

I arrived home, and as I made my way down the garden I could just make out her shape, as I got closer I saw her. There are no words to describe seeing your child lying there so still, so lifeless. I held her and desperately begged her to open her eyes. Oh, why Sinead? A member of the ambulance crew who had arrived earlier was crying. They turned away to allow us some privacy, and despite my pleadings with Sinead, she was gone. I studied her face, her freckles, her little diamond stud at the side of her nose. The one I had given out about only a few short months ago. The ambulance crew were waiting to take Sinead away for a post-mortem. I had to let them take her. I warned them *no* one is to remove that little diamond stud. I think I probably stressed that to them more than once. I wonder is it possible to actually hear a heart break.

I went inside to face our children. I walked into the sitting room, where they sat in stunned silence. Donal and myself desperately wanted to find some wise words, to comfort and console, but there were no words. How could we help them make sense of this, when we couldn't make any sense of it ourselves? I thought something like this only happens to other people. How had this happened to Sinead?

Neighbours, friends, family all made their way to our home. Shock and horror etched on their faces. Sinead's grandmothers sat on the sofa together just holding one another. They each had a special name for Sinead since she was a tot. Donal's mother Kay called her 'my lovely one', my mother Rita called her 'Petal'.

We were all so devastated that Sinead could have felt despair so intense that it had led to her ending her life. I searched and searched for a suicide note; I felt certain she would have left one somewhere. I so desperately needed to understand what had been going on in her mind that day, but there was no note, no goodbyes. Was it only two weeks ago on Mother's Day that Sinead had brought up breakfast in bed for me? She had cut toast into the shape of the letters *I luv u*, and she had a poem she had written for me. Neighbours, family friends, and the whole community, it seemed, called to offer their condolences and support. They cleaned, cooked, brought food, anything people felt they could do to help, they did.

Finally Sinead was brought home. So many teenagers called over the next couple of days, classmates and pals who called to say their final goodbyes to their friend Sinead, and to help and support David, Thomas, and Eimear. They brought cards, wrote poems, and told wonderful stories of their friendships with Sinead over the years. We found some consolation in their presence. They were so open, thoughtful and considerate. We laughed and cried with them, and every one of them holds a special place in our hearts. We will be forever grateful to everyone.

Eimear was still only seven years old, and was often to be found just sitting beside Sinead's body just chatting away to her. I called her one morning for a little breakfast. As she ran down the stairs she shouted to me: 'I'll be there in a minute, mam. I just want to go into the sitting room and say good morning to Sinead.'

Just before the funeral, Eimear went outside to the garden. She returned with handfuls of cherry-blossom petals, and gently sprinkled them over Sinead. Our hearts broke for Eimear. She had lost her big sister, her heroine. David and Thomas each wrote letters to their sister and laid them gently beside her. The funeral passed in a haze. Sinead's dad gave a moving eulogy to his beloved daughter. Then came the pain of turning away from the grave, and leaving Sinead alone.

The first couple of days after the funeral were somewhat of a relief for me. Just to not have to face so many people in the house. We were all truly exhausted. I think we all went to the four corners of the house. We felt so grateful for all the support, but now we needed time to be alone, to grieve.

As the days passed, the full reality of this awful tragedy became brutally apparent.

Oh! Those early days of unspeakable pain.

The cruel sight of Sinead's empty bed, day after day, so neat, so tidy. That silence that went on and on. Her bedroom had always been so noisy and a little untidy, a normal teenager's bedroom; where loud music played constantly, as girls sang along, giggling as they tried out make-up and perfume, sometimes while straightening each other's hair. That hair straightener was one of Sinead's prized possessions. She had her curly hair straightened to within an inch of its life every day before she would leave the house.

How many times had I complained to her: 'Tidy your room turn the music down, keep the noise down.' Oh! regrets. The very things I nagged about were now the things I missed most of all. Oh! Sticking her chewing gum in the fridge, I even missed that. I went over and over past conversations I had with her trying to find clues for what had happened. Had I said anything to upset her? Had I been too lenient with her? Had I been too strict? Had I been overprotective? Had I told her enough how much I loved her?

Why hadn't I woken her up that final morning to check how she was? Why? Why?

Some days, such heartache can take away the will to keep on going, but we had our other children to care for, to love, and to keep safe. They were going through the same grief that we were, and I knew they were trying to be strong for us. Life had taken on a fragility for me, and I hated leaving my teenage sons even for short spells. There was always that scary moment of entering the house. If it was too quiet, my heart would skip a few beats. My first thoughts would be: 'Are they okay?'

People were generally extremely kind and supportive. Unfortunately sometimes, through not knowing what to say, or an inability to handle our grief, a few people inadvertently caused crushing pain by using comments such as: 'You're lucky you have three other children', 'You'll get over it', 'You have an angel in heaven', 'You'll never have to worry about her again' or 'It could have been worse.' I don't wish to sound harsh, and people may feel that there really is nothing too wrong in what these people said, but I would say, when a child dies and particularly in those early days when your feelings of loss are so raw, and you feel so grief-stricken, all you want is your child back, not some perfect angel in heaven. I just wanted my not-so-perfect angel here with me. So please don't let another kind person say to me: 'I understand how you feel.' If you have not lost a child you cannot understand how I feel, and I truly hope you never will.

What I found gave comfort was just a touch on the shoulder, the holding of a hand, or just to say: 'I don't know what to say.' It really is all anyone needs to do and you actually don't even need to say anything at all, because if you have love and compassion in your heart it will shine through and give comfort. I slowly began to find it more and more difficult to go out. I felt people were staring at me, judging me as I passed by. I felt they were thinking what could have made a young girl end her own life in such a way. What kind of mother was I really? I wanted to scream I loved my daughter. We had a very close relationship. We are a close family. These feelings are all very common in families who are bereaved by suicide. I think people are probably so terrified of suicide that they start looking at you, almost as if studying you, hoping to find reasons why it couldn't possibly happen to their families. I'm sure in the past I've done this very same thing.

I have learned there are no short cuts through the grieving process. Anger and guilt, for me, were the two emotions I battled with. A friend asked me was I angry at Sinead and I can honestly say I only ever felt love and compassion for her. I knew she had obviously been more desperately unwell than any of us realised. People who are in a depressed state can hide their feelings behind that mask we all wear. Smiles can hide so much pain. No, the only anger I ever felt was aimed at myself. As time has gone by, that anger has diminished and in its place is now a sense of regret. Anger turned inwards is a destructive force. As it's probably impossible in life to live without feelings of guilt, a part of what makes us human, I have found a little space inside of myself where I keep these two emotions in check. As humans we all make mistakes and sadly we have many limitations. I've had to come to terms with some of mine, but beyond this comes forgiveness for ourselves and others.

I found wonderful and essential help and support through counselling I attended on an ongoing basis for many months. For me it was a safe place where I could talk, cry, and rage at the world. My GP had recommended this wonderful counsellor. He has been there for me and all the family at different stages. Even now he still rings to check how everybody is doing, and we have a bit of a chat. He has been of enormous help to us all and we will never forget his kindness. To us he is more a family friend than a counsellor. Friends and family have been wonderful but a professional ear is of such great benefit. Don't be afraid to reach out for help, if you need it. There is no shame.

I still found the quietness in our house very difficult. and a friend (actually it was the aforementioned counsellor) suggested getting a dog. I thought he was mad but the more I thought about it the more I felt maybe it wouldn't be such a bad idea, especially for Eimear who was still missing her sister. Now I know this probably would not be the best of ideas for other people, as dogs need a lot of care and attention, walks, etc, ... and other people may not have the energy or enthusiasm for taking care of any pets at this time, but one particular Saturday morning we all piled into the car and off we went to look at a litter of chocolate Labradors. There we met and fell in love with a beautiful little brown pup.

Eimear soon made it quite clear he was going to be her puppy. His registration papers were made out in Eimear's name, and she called him Max. She fell in love instantly with her new best friend. He is a gorgeous, big, gentle giant of a dog who has only ever given us all buckets of unconditional love from his earliest days with us. I started taking him for walks; as he grew these walks became very, very long walks. Out to the nearby woods we would head. Often I would sit for a rest with Max beside me. I'd cry and sob and Max would look at me as if to say: 'I know.' I'd hug him and off we'd go again. These walks helped to lift my spirits so much. The simplest pleasures in life can help to lift the heaviest hearts. Since then, three more dogs have joined the pack, but Max is still so special. My eldest son David is now the official dog walker of the family, but I still borrow them from time to time.

Slowly, we have picked up the shattered pieces of our lives. Our children continue to help make every day worth living. Life once more holds many joys. Family holidays and meals out with my noisy bunch are a treat. We are able to embrace life, laughter and fun once more. I love being in their company and I know they love being in the company of each other. Sinead's spirit is forever present amongst us and no more so than when we are laughing heartily or when her sister Eimear is gleefully teasing her poor auld dad. Although there is always a sense of sadness in our hearts at the manner of her lonely death, we honour her memory by remembering her and celebrating her life.

Some wonderful people have come into our lives since Sinead's death. Some briefly and some have become firm friends. I have heard many peoples' stories of love and loss, so many brave, resilient people who live amongst us. It never ceases to amaze me just how strong the human spirit is.

All of life's experiences change us for good or bad, it's how we choose to deal with these changes that show our true character, but it does all take time.

We as a family feel privileged and grateful to have had Sinead in our lives for sixteen years. She entered our world and enriched our lives for ever. We feel blessed to have known her, loved her and felt her love for us. Her death affected so many people: parents, brothers, sister, grandparents, aunts, uncles, cousins, friends and teachers. The ripples extended outwards.

So many people are affected by suicide in this country. Ten people at least die by suicide every week in Ireland, eight males and two females, all loved and cherished by families and friends. No matter what the problem, there is always help available. There are always choices in the type of help you would wish to have: GP, counselling, addiction services, Samaritans, reach out to a friend or family member. The very, very worst choice anyone can make is suicide.

Will I ever see Sinead again? I don't know. I don't have too many definite answers anymore, but I like to think I will, and if I do I have many questions for her. But you know, I think I would probably just put them all aside, because my dream is just to hold her for the longest time. *Grá mo chroí.*

Help me to know my loved one is with the Great Spirit and has found rest and peace. One day we will be reunited, but until then, I ask for help to keep going on in life.
Prayer by Brave Heart, Native American Shaman

Our Angel & Gladiator

Once upon a time, I had two beautiful daughters, one born an angel and the other a gladiator. Being a mother was the best job, and even though I had many different careers, it was the one I loved the most. We had such fun: the parties, the sleepovers, and the picnics.

Sarah was my first-born, strong, beautiful and full of integrity. One of the first words she spoke was 'horse' and she had her first lesson at the age of three and a half. She loved animals and there is hardly a domestic pet I haven't cared for in the last twenty years: dogs, rabbits, hamsters, turtles, birds, goldfish and, of course, horses. Sarah lived life at a fast pace, she never seemed to slow down, always chasing the next idea. She was very black and white in her thinking, and God help you if you got on the wrong side of her. However, she was also a great friend and, after she died, I learnt from her friends how much she had done to help them when they needed support. I found this out for myself when Kate, my other daughter, was sick. Sarah was such a support both emotionally and practically, but more of that later. My husband and I always said that we got a daughter each. Sarah was his – they had this connection where words were not even necessary. They both loved cars and it was many a Sunday they would both head off to a rally. She was driving on her own at the age of ten and her dad taught her, through motorsport, the dangers of driving on the road. How ironic that she should die in a car she wasn't even driving.

Four years later, and Kate came into our lives. This cherub-faced child drew the attention of many a stranger, so much so that I used to worry that she would die or maybe go missing. But as she got older, I became more relaxed. Kate had a gift of making you feel good no matter what age you were. She had an ability to understand how you were feeling and to say the right thing. She adored Sarah – she was her hero – and when she went into secondary school she was always grateful that she had a big sister to protect her from the bullies. Sarah, on the other hand, could take or leave Kate, suddenly having a younger sister following you around all day, having to share things with, wasn't all that great. My favourite memory of the early days is when they would be in the back of the car and you would hear a shout: 'Mum, tell her to stop looking at me!' Kate and I had a lot in common, we both liked and shared the finer things in life: music, food, shopping, art, the list goes on. We spent hours giving each other back rubs, facials, manicures. She too had a love for animals and nature. She also had a pony, the only difference being that while Sarah wanted to jump the highest fence, Kate wanted to win the best-turned-out rider and pony.

On 12 September 2005, Kate was diagnosed with cancer. It was a Monday and David had taken her for an x-ray. She had a pain in her groin and we thought she had hurt herself horse riding. I was at work, so David was on his own when the doctor pointed out this large mass with concern in his voice and suggested that she be taken straight away to Crumlin Children's Hospital. I didn't go to the hospital that evening. I stayed and organised Sarah because even then I knew we were in trouble, this was the start of a long journey. The next morning a good friend drove me there. To this day I can't remember the journey. After a couple of days and many tests it was confirmed that Kate had a rare bone cancer called *'Ewing's Sarcoma'* in the joint of her hip. On Friday she was let home for the weekend and we were to arrive back on the ward on Monday morning to be hooked up for chemotherapy. During the weekend David and I decided to introduce and explain the word 'cancer'. We didn't want Kate to be afraid so we answered all her questions truthfully. We told her about friends of ours who had survived cancer and that it wasn't necessary to be afraid.

We discovered that when people are uncomfortable with an illness, they say inappropriate things which can hurt your feelings. Kate and I decided to keep a diary of all the stupid things people said to her. For example, after she had lost all her hair from chemotherapy, someone said to her one day: 'I'll get out of your hair and see you later!' You may find this story strange but Kate was only thirteen years old and, by keeping this diary, we turned many a negative situation into a positive one by having a laugh.

Kate lived through almost two years of treatment, chemotherapy, radiation and major surgery in England. It was the first
time that this procedure had been performed. We had to sign papers confirming that we were aware that our daughter could die
on the operating theatre, and, if not there, possibly from infection
afterwards. When the time came for Kate to go to theatre, it was
Sarah who held her hand until she went to sleep, 'The Gladiator'.

Kate didn't die. She survived after a hip replacement and her
pelvis being removed, radiated and replaced. It was a medical
breakthrough and we would be asked later for our permission
for the surgery to be entered into the medical journals. Kate and I
stayed in that hospital for several weeks afterwards, with David
and Sarah along with family and friends flying over at the weekends. Kate had to learn to walk again, she had sixty-eight staples
and six stitches. When her wound healed, she would show it to
friends and joke that she had been bitten by a shark. When David
and I first met the surgeon, he said one important thing to us: 'I
can remove your daughter's tumour, but I can't guarantee that
she won't die from cancer.' At least he was honest, and on 28 July
2007 in the arms of her dad, Kate passed away peacefully. I spent
two years fighting to keep my child alive and during that time I
could not afford to grieve for her, for Sarah and David. It was just
a case of survival.

So much happened during that time. Sarah did her Leaving
Certificate, got her driver's licence, made her debs and she fell in
love. All of this was sidelined by this demon called cancer, and
whilst David struggled along trying to make a living and attempting to keep us all positive, it was the most difficult time in
our marriage, and we are together a long time. In Kate's final
days she needed round-the-clock care and only for Sarah I don't
know what I would have done. She drove up and down to
Crumlin hospital with blood samples, she did Kate's medication
when I needed a rest or just time to have a shower. As a family
we had many a discussion about death and how we would like
Kate to be remembered. So when it came to Kate's funeral, we
had it planned long in advance. This is probably one of the only
advantages of a terminal illness: it gives you time to sort out your
life and to plan things the way you would want. We never told

Kate that she was dying but I think that she had come to realise that she might be, so she wrote to some of her friends and made a point of talking to her best friend a couple of days before she died. Kate had a wonderful life and she inspired so many people to do better. Her funeral was attended by hundreds and it was one of the most wonderful celebrations of life I've ever seen or attended. For some of her friends, this was the first time they lost somebody they loved so we encouraged them all to visit our house while she was laid out. Her boyfriend, who had been on holidays and never got to give her the designer handbag he got her, was so upset that I suggested he write her a letter and put it in the bag and that we would bury it with her. In the end I think almost every child who knew her, wrote her a note. I looked out the window and they were all in different groups sitting on the grass sharing paper and pens and swapping stories.

On the day of her funeral, we had a bunch of pink balloons on the church altar, as a symbol of the celebration, and after the burial Sarah released them to the sounds of *'True Colours'*. Kate was buried on a Tuesday and on the Wednesday Sarah had jumped into protection mode as she hovered around trying to support myself and David. I can't remember much of the next week: I think the exhaustion was finally catching up, but I do remember Sarah crawling into our bed one morning to have a chat about the future. Herself and Jason, her boyfriend, had been thinking of travelling and would David and I mind. She was worried about Kate's dog who had been very upset and lonely and should she get another to keep him company. David and I were numb but we were functioning. The house was still like a revolving door with family and friends calling with food and support. The four of us were discussing our plans to organise a pink memorial ball in Kate's honour for Crumlin hospital. David and I were going to form an adult committee; Sarah and Jason, a youth committee.

On Thursday, Sarah arrived home with a new hairstyle, a new look, a new beginning. Her friends were taking her and Jason out for a few drinks the following night, so they were going to park up the car and stay over. On Saturday the four of us were invited to a party. However, at around 11.00 a.m. Sarah phoned to say she was still in bed and was exhausted after the night before so she was going to come home with Jason and they were going to skip the party. She asked if I would get some steaks in for later. I went to Naas to do the shopping and I met David for lunch. During lunch, Sarah rang again to say that she had found a dog to keep Kate's dog company and how did I feel about it. I told her I loved her and that we would discuss it when I got home. David went on to call in on a friend whose garage was on the way home and I went home to have a nap before the Christening party. At 2.00 p.m. David received a phone call to say that Sarah had been in a car accident near our house and as he pulled out from the garage, the fire-brigade went by. He arrived at the accident scene to discover Jason being lifted into an ambulance but Sarah was trapped in the wreckage. Even though our house is only a quarter of a mile away, I heard nothing. David arrived soon afterwards with Sarah's friend and they told me that Sarah had been in an accident and that we needed to go to the hospital. I couldn't believe it. It had to be a mistake, not my Sarah, sure hadn't I talked to her a while ago. When we arrived at the hospital, there were people I knew everywhere including Jason's family. Everybody was acting very strangely but what I didn't know was that Sarah was dead and that David couldn't bring himself to tell me. He had watched as her life drained away from her as the emergency services cut her from the car. Word spread so fast, we were under pressure to inform our families.

We arrived home later that afternoon to a house full of the same people, the same women making tea with the same cups and boiler that had been used two weeks earlier to the day that Kate had died. My brain was screaming 'How can we do this again?' I had months to plan Kate's funeral, how can I do justice to Sarah in three days? It was during Kate's illness that I realised that she was born an angel, not just her but all the children in the cancer ward. Through their pain we are made better people and we are taught life lessons that we will never forget. In that moment I realised that I would cope with Sarah's death and funeral because Kate had taught me how. So yet again, on a Tuesday morning David and I walked behind the coffin of our daughter, this time followed by press and photographers. The country was in shock, how could life be so cruel, two beautiful children dead in two weeks?

The brain is a wonderful thing and I now realise that it only allows you to process a certain amount of grief at a time. In the first year we were in shock and I have few memories except that we went ahead with the memorial ball as a tribute to both of the girls and we had it on their first anniversary. It was wonderful, and a reason for their families and friends to get together on their first anniversary. We also went on to participate in a TV ad for the Road Safety Authority, and I have become a volunteer with the Irish Cancer Society helping women with cancer.

David and I have struggled over the last few years to come to terms with each other's pain, to learn to live as a childless couple again, to focus and create a new life without our children. As a woman you take for granted having children. We forget that sometimes it is not possible, maybe through death or infertility, but still we are asked: 'How many children do you have?' when we are introduced to someone new. When you have lost a child, that's a hard one to answer. I have lost my children but I have also lost the chance of a son-in-law and grandchildren. Having spoken with other bereaved people, I have come to realise that one of the healing factors in grief is recognition of that grief in the first place. We had hundreds at Kate's funeral and thousands at Sarah's, and to this day, not a day goes by that someone doesn't mention them. I believe this to mean that they mattered. For a time afterwards, David and I couldn't talk, worried that we would burden each other with our pain. However, that has changed and now we can talk openly about the girls and our feelings. Each day is a little better, not because the pain gets less – it doesn't – but you get stronger. You have to live each day as if it is your last, because after watching someone you love fight for each precious minute, you don't put life on hold.

Hip Hop Legacy

Neevin met Megan, my daughter, at school in his thirteenth year. They sang in the choir together and 'hung out' in the teenage vernacular. Neevin had joined the choir thinking he was going to learn to rap: a popular youth music/dance genre consisting of chanted, often improvised, street poetry accompanied by a collage of well-known music recordings and mixes. Much to his surprise he ended up singing rather traditional tunes.

Neevin was a very likeable person. We saw him often. He often arrived at our house just around dinner time.

I got to know Neevin well and became very fond of him. He was very musical, had a good sense of humour, a strong sense of optimism and a good heart. I mentored him on any number of topics relevant to a young man growing up, encouraging him to complete his education. We got on well.

At seventeen years, Megan surprised us by becoming pregnant. It was obvious some of my counselling hadn't worked. Devon Jacob Rampersad Tracy was born … a spitting image of Neevin.

Megan and Neevin were together two years but drifted apart. Devon stayed with Megan and much to my chagrin, Neevin was very erratic in his seeing and attending to his new son. I persevered and kept in touch with Neevin, continuing with the mentoring whenever I could. I also spent a lot of time with Devon becoming surrogate father and Grandpa T.

The moment is etched in my mind and soul. The telephone call from Megan, on that very cold December day seven days before Christmas, was numbing: 'Neevin is dead. He froze to death', she cried, 'He left his car after it stalled in the blizzard last night.' My mind went blank as I tried to comprehend the message. This wasn't happening. She reiterated the message again: 'Neevin is dead, dad … he froze to death after leaving his stalled car.' That evening was the coldest winter night on record and was accompanied by a major snow storm. Tears rolled down my

63

cheeks. I said as best I could: 'I will be right over', as I struggled through a growing well of tears to find the next exit. I can still hear myself saying: 'Neevin, Neevin, Why? Why? Why?' over and over again. 'You were only 25, you had a whole life ahead of you!' My mind shifted to Devon: 'Devon is without a father,' I said to myself out loud. This one point hit terribly hard. I had seen Neevin a week earlier when he attended Devon's birthday party. He had taken the initiative to tell me he was going to see Devon more often, had a new apartment and a new job for the New Year and things were really looking up. I was emotionally reminded and shaken the next day as the event was published on the front page of our local newspaper with a full-sized picture of Neevin. The feelings one has at the event of death are private in oneself. No one can feel the depth of sorrow and emptiness one feels in experiencing the moment. The experience takes all of one's inner resources to manage. Friends and relatives are helpful but the full import of the experience is left to the one experiencing the event. I was numb and disorientated. I loved that young man in my own way. Now he was gone. My faith held me well. I spoke to God: 'Please, Lord, provide for Neevin as he enters your kingdom.' One has to believe in something larger than 'self' to give context to and receive support in such traumatic circumstances. It does not take away the emptiness and pain, but provides a way to move through the process of self-healing and new beginnings.

The funeral was very difficult for me as I saw and experienced the love for Neevin expressed by many people, young and old. Neevin's mother was not present, having succumbed to alcoholism a few years earlier. I found myself sobbing as I watched friends Neevin's age contribute to the service in many ways using verse and music that Neevin enjoyed. 'Neevin will no longer be a part of this group physically but will be in soul and spirit', I thought. It did not take away that emptiness entirely but provided some consolation for a difficult time. Devon, now seven years old, and his Mom visited with Neevin at the front of the chapel. I truly believe Megan loved Neevin, in a relationship that was not to be. Throughout the service I held Devon. I recall

him saying: 'I 'm not going to cry', as I cried. Two burning questions nagged at me: 'What about Devon?' and 'What about
Megan?' What do we need to do to ensure they are supported in
the years to come? ... a father's question and a grandfather's
question in the same breath. Neevin was buried beside his mother. His father died suddenly a short time later, leaving behind
one brother and a sister with whom we maintain special contact
to this day.

Without hesitation, we got on with the business of doing: the
easy part; and trying to 'be': the tough part. It was very difficult
in the first year as we relived family events one by one-
Christmas, Easter, birthdays, Sunday dinners and so on, without
Neevin's presence. Christmas was and still is the most difficult of
times because Neevin was buried shortly before Christmas in
that fateful year. The memories come flooding back vividly but
with lesser emotional intensity as the years go by. My heart aches
watching Megan's tears and quiet reflection as she experiences
'Neevin moments'.

While we have cried, we have laughed as well. Of particular
note was Neevin's habit of wearing socks in the lake at our cottage so as not to get his feet 'yucky'. Devon does the same thing,
yet has not had an ounce of instruction from anyone; genetic
legacy maybe?

Megan, being a single mother, struggled with getting back on
track. She is strong and self-willed and resilient which has held her
in good stead over the years. Devon became my 'Best Buddy'. I
have followed his progress carefully at school, coached him along
the way, (once a teacher, always a teacher!) signed him up for soc-
cer, piano lessons, baseball and basketball, made sure he got to his
games with the right equipment, took him fishing and to our
'boys-work weekends' at the cottage. We also took him and
Megan on our various travels to the US, Mexico and Europe.

A turning point came when he was thirteen and he was ad-
judged to be too small to play Rep basketball, which was disap-
pointing for him. Undaunted, Devon said he would like to do
Hip Hop dancing and go to Los Angeles someday, something he
could see his father doing. A flashback! He was seven when his

father passed and I thought he might not have as much recollection of the event at thirteen. The memories and emotions surfaced and came flooding back. I quietly wiped the tears from my eyes once more; this time, not as much in sorrow, but in joy and celebration of a Father's legacy. We embarked on a three year, two nights a week practices and weekend competition odyssey in which Devon became more and more proficient and was being publically recognised for his talent.

Devon has shown a determination, and the creativity, to master the art of dance and subsequently 'rap'. When asked what makes him successful, he quietly and humbly says 'hard work'. What he doesn't tell you is he writes his own material and practices continuously to improve his 'style'.

His *YouTube* appearances under 'Devon Tracy' and 'thadancerkidd' have attracted thousands of views.

As I write this, Devon is in Los Angeles with a six month contract to perform. His music is being played on regional radio stations in Canada and the US. Devon said to me as he headed off to Los Angeles that 'he thought his future lay in the music business' in some capacity. The dancing and rapping was a good *entrée* into the business which could lead to managing other performers. He has a vision of his future which while somewhat unclear at the moment will crystallise as he experiences the journey and 'works hard' at acquiring the skills and ability to define his career success.

I am very proud of Devon as my grandson and 'Best Buddy', and Megan as my daughter and the mother of Devon, Taya and Jordan. It has been more than ten years since Neevin's passing. His spirit lives on in Devon which is of great consolation to us all.

Our difficult memories of Neevin's death will continue with us throughout life while the more deeply felt emotions become more temporal. We rejoice in the here and now while allowing ourselves the quiet moments of reflection and tears invoked by current-past connectors. We know intrinsically that we have been charged with the responsibility of adding daily value to others through the legacy left by Neevin and now being carried forward by Devon.

As I reflect upon the overall experience, I know that 'faith in

God, faith in self and faith in others coupled with trust in God, trust in self and trust in others' is the equation which has allowed me to move on and move forward in difficult times.

The irony in death is that there is life. Life takes on a different complexion as we make our own accommodation for traumatic events and have the option of dwelling or moving on to learn, grow and be strengthened from the experience, so that we may support others and live out our full potential in the grace of God.

A Walk In My Shoes

The greatest Love came by today
And swiftly stole my son away
'It's time' the whisper as he slept
And gently drew him into death.

These words describe for me two things, the first is the greatest act of mercy and love I have known and the second is the deepest pain and struggle of a life filled with many struggles. Let me tell you the story of the beloved son who is at the centre of these quite conflicting events, and what I have learnt, if anything.

Derek was born in 1976, the fifth of my children and the third with cystic fibrosis. This is a life-threatening disease and life expectancy is, in Ireland, late twenties or maximum early thirties. Derek achieved thirty-two years. However, this gloomy prognosis does not even begin to describe who he was or what his life was like.

He was a very loving but intensely private person who never wanted to be given any special privileges because of his illness. Very few of his large circle of friends and colleagues knew of his cystic fibrosis and diabetes and it came as quite a shock to them when he died.

Because of his frequent stays in hospital as a child, he was much closer to his dad and I than would normally be the case. From the earliest days he and I developed a bond of friendship and acceptance of each other which was truly unusual. He was funny and quirky and so generous with his time and affection to everyone who knew him. However, I do not want you to think he was some sort of goody-two-shoes. Not a bit of it, he was always willing to do anything and try everything, a lot of which we only discovered after his death. Just as well!

When he was a child he used to call his sister, Elaine, his 'second Mammy'. Elaine was five years old when Derek was born and, being a typical little girl and Derek being so tiny, she used to mind him and cuddle him. His favourite time with Elaine was, when he was unwell, she would sit on the sofa and he would put his head on her lap and she would stroke his hair. Looking back now, I am amazed that a little girl would sit for ages gently stroking her brother's head and forehead, for love's sake. Derek remembered this well into adulthood and it was a precious memory for him I know. He and his brother had quite a different relationship, a very normal brotherly one I imagine – they pummelled each other unmercifully, as boys do. Why is it that boys seem to have this overwhelming urge to be physical? Refereeing was a full-time occupation with those two.

As teenagers and into adulthood they were very close, bonded together by their love of music and guitars. Many a time, the neighbours were bombarded with their attempts to emulate Bon Jovi and other famous rock bands. My garage became the sound stage for their efforts for several years. It was just as well I loved rock music myself and never really noticed the noise levels.

Derek went on to make music and sound his full-time career. Indeed I could honestly say that music was his life. He played guitar all his life and one of the things I miss most of all is the constant guitar strumming coming from the upstairs room. He travelled all over the country and abroad doing sound for concerts, conferences, etc, during the years his health was good and, from what I have been told, was not averse to madcap adventuring in the process. If he was hospitalised, which happened frequently, and he was required to do a gig (event) he would simply agree to do it, not divulging his whereabouts, proceed to tell the nurse he was just slipping out to the shop and would then go ahead (cannula in his arm and a sock over it to hide it) and sneak back into the hospital at three o'clock in the morning when he had finished. As this happened regularly, the nurses came to realise what he was up to and there was an unspoken agreement that neither party would admit to foreknowledge.

In his last year, we could see very clearly that he was losing his battle and it was a very tough year for him, and for us. His diabetes went out of control and his lungs deteriorated steadily. His whole body started breaking down and he was literally dying on his feet but still he asked for no quarter.

Over the years, because of our closeness, I had come to admire Derek greatly and I am not ashamed to say that he had become a role model for me in my life. The love we shared meant that we had, from early on, developed a very strong empathy toward each other and this in his last months grew ever stronger. Feelings were shared without the need for words and we each knew the end was near.

As a mother what could I do? This for me was a time of great conflict and helplessness as it was for him. He was of course very bitter for a time because of his impending death and I watched helplessly as he fought the good fight towards acceptance. One of his worries I know was about me. How do I know? It was one of the last conversations we had and I, for love's sake, told him he must live *his* life and I had to walk my path. Little did I know that day that I was letting him go forever.

I remember the Wednesday before he died, lying in bed listening to him coughing and vomiting in the bathroom. I was crying as I pleaded with God to help him. I remember saying: 'It is so unfair, he has suffered enough, please, please help him.' He did, by letting him gently fall asleep and die during that sleep just a few days later. God waited just long enough for us to have the conversation and I could say, for the last time, 'Go ahead, son, it is your life and you must live it for you and I must live mine.'

I never believed that emotional pain could be so strong as to become physical but it does and it did. His death was a wrenching of my soul and although it was expected, it was still the most horrendous shock. Just how much he was entwined in our very existence only became clear when he was no longer there.

In the beginning, when the adrenalin surge of coping with the arrangements and the hundreds of friends, family and well-wishers, who I must say came from far and wide, kept us going, it was not too bad. It was as if there was a conspiracy to do everything possible, and do it well, in order to ensure Derek knew how much he was loved and to make him proud. When this died down as, inevitably, people returned to their lives and the long, lonely days without him began, I was convinced I could not do this. I could not go on, it was one blow too many, the only thing that kept me putting one foot in front of another was the love I felt, and still feel, for my husband, son, daughter and grandchildren. I could not be the cause of them suffering even more. They had been through so much with Derek dying.

During that first year, all sorts of things were constantly going through my mind: 'Did I do enough for him? Was I loving enough? Why didn't I know that he would die that day?' And many other such thoughts. Not unusual I know, but very hard to get through. I also learned that, like death itself, grief is a path that you walk alone, no matter how loving your family or friends, because as individuals grief manifests itself differently in each one of us. The pain and loss are caused by the same event but our reactions are different and that makes it a lonely struggle.

The big one for me was: 'Is he happy? What if there's nothing there and heaven is not real?' I had always believed in life after death but now it took on a whole new meaning for me. Because I loved my son so much I worried that he was not happy. He deserved more than just an end to suffering, he deserved peace.

I had always had a strong faith but now it seemed I needed, being the type of person I am, to try and see things from a different perspective. For most of us, loving our children is as natural as breathing, as is our desire to 'make smooth their paths'. Easy when they are small, not always easy when they are independent adults and yet we still love them passionately. What do we love? We love their very existence, the very essence of their being, we no longer really see their physicality, it is deeper than that. I, very slowly and over much time, began to realise that this is what, for me, is at the heart of Christianity, the love of the very essence of humanity. It answers for me the question of how one could lay down his life for another in love. That which animates the physical and shines out of the eyes of each one of us, that which makes us so unique and individual, that is the essence of humanity.

Call it what you will – the soul, the spirit – whatever, that is what we grow to love in each other and that, to me, is what God loves. Yes my son is physically gone and I will never again gaze upon his beloved face and the pain of his going still hurts and probably always will. Hopefully I will learn to live my life beside that great emptiness. What keeps me going is that I still feel the warmth of his loving, funny, brave spirit and I believe that for as long as the wind blows and the sun shines, plants flower, die and regrow, my son's spirit will be at one with that great, diverse, unknowable life force we call God. This is what keeps me moving forward so that when my time comes and I too join that unending stream, I will once again meet my son and my Maker to love and live in the spirit.

A Letter to Nicholas

Dear Nicholas,

I have been asked to write about you, but first I wanted to write *to* you. It seems strange because everyday I think of you and say your name in my head. You are always my little tiny baby. But today I realise as I write this letter that you would have been a young man of nearly twenty-four. I see your brother Ashley and your sister Sophie and realise how much of life you missed, my precious darling.

The day you were born, Sunday 5 April, was, I recall, sunny. I lay in bed and realised that you had not woken me up that night with your kicking. I felt nervous and told your dad. He immediately rang the hospital. I had been on bedrest for the past two weeks because at thirty weeks I had suffered *placenta prevea* whilst we were on holiday in Devon, staying with friends at their farm in Branscombe. The setting was idyllic. I was the happiest woman in the world. What your father and I did not realise then was that this idyll was soon to come crashing in around us. I was rushed into Exeter Hospital.

I was petrified. I knew if you came this early it would not be good for you. But the bleeding stopped and the medical staff reassured me that you were safe and sound. The sun was shining on that day also. I relaxed and all seemed well with the world. After a couple of days, dad drove us back to London. I felt every bump even though he drove with caution. He had a very precious package on board. You. But you were safe in my tummy.

As I had been instructed, I took to my bed for complete bedrest and ate my way through tons of chocolate. They told me to keep a 'kick chart' which I completed diligently. You kicked for Britain. We joked that you would play for England. All was well with the world.

But on that sunny Sunday morning in our lovely little house in East Ham I knew something was terribly wrong. My tummy had been still for too long now. Dad drove us to Newham General. There was a sense of urgency on the ward when they

73

admitted me. I was really scared. This was not how it was meant to be. We had planned and waited so patiently for you.

The doctor gave me an ultrasound that seemed to last forever. My tummy hurt because he kept pressing on the same area. He said he was sorry but that something was wrong. He said you had suffered a heart attack. This was crazy. What on earth was he saying? He must be wrong. My dad, your grandad died at fifty-three (not at all old, now that I am fifty-three!) with a heart attack. Heart attacks only happen to old people, don't they? I remember my head was spinning – I felt delirious.

The doctor told your Dad and me that they had to perform an emergency caesarean. I was so scared but I remember thinking that I must keep calm for your sake. I did not want to make you more sick. Dad asked if we could wait to see if you got better. How naive we were. The doctor said no.

They let your dad come into theatre with me just before they put me out. I remember he had tears streaming down his face. They had made him gown up and he had a floral hat on which resembled a shower cap. I remember smiling because it looked funny. How strange life is when you are in the scariest situation of your life and then you see something that makes you smile. I prayed hard. I was scared and frightened. As I drifted off the last thing I saw was your dad's face looking just as scared and frightened.

I could hear voices. Lots of them. Gradually I was able to differentiate between them. I heard your dad saying through his sobs: 'We have a boy, Lynda, a little boy.' I felt so proud to have a son. I realised then that although I had told everyone I did not mind what I had just so long as the baby was healthy, deep down I had wanted a son. I heard your Nan saying: 'Be brave darling.' Why? Then the doctor saying: 'I am sorry but your son has *spina bifida*. He had tears in his eyes. What was happening? Surely they had made a mistake.

You lived your short little life in a glass incubator in the Special Baby Care Unit. You looked perfect to us. But they kept saying there was something wrong with you. Well, not to us. The doctors came from The Royal London Hospital. They said it was genetic. How did they know?

They took a photo of you laying there with all those tubes. It seemed wrong. They told your Dad to go home and get his camera. He obeyed. He described driving home in the car to collect the camera as feeling like he was in a gold fish bowl. It all seemed too tragic. But those little photos of you are so precious to us because they are all we have left of you.

You died in my arms when you were just twelve precious hours old. They knew how poorly you had become and they gently took you out of the incubator. You were so tiny. I loved you so much. We loved you so much. My heart broke. It has never healed.

They took you to the Chapel of Rest and they took me back to my bed. I felt so lonely even though I was surrounded by family. My body ached for you. All I had was this searing wound in my tummy where I felt they had torn you from me, and a cuddly lion toy that your Auntie Maria had put on top of the incubator. We called him Lenny the Lion-heart. He was meant to help you fight for your tiny little life. I guess he just was not strong enough darling.

I was in a blurred world. Nothing seemed real anymore only the scar from the caesarean. I remember being taken to the Chapel of Rest with your dad. They had laid you out in a pretty little Moses basket. Very similar to the one we had waiting at home for you in the nursery. I kissed you. You were so cold. This surprised me. I had never been near a dead body before. Deep inside me I was screaming – my baby cannot be dead. But nobody could hear me.

Life became a haze. They kept me in a side-room away from the other new mums. I felt like a leper. Then one day they came to talk about funeral arrangements. You had been baptised in the Special Baby Care Unit. Nanny Jessie and grandad Fred were your Godparents. We arranged to have you buried with your grandad Charles. Every ounce of my body was screaming out and nobody could hear me. Why my baby?

They sent your tiny little body to Great Ormond St. They said it was best if there was an autopsy. So that we would know what was wrong for any future children. We believed them. I was scared that you were on your own and that they might lose you.

In fact they did worse if that is possible. They stole your organs for medical research and never asked our permission. They sent your beautiful little body back a shell. We only discovered many years later what they had done to you. I am so sorry my darling. I should have looked after you better.

Your funeral was on Maundy Thursday 17 April. It was sunny that Easter, apparently but I didn't notice. I wish I could say that I took comfort in knowing that you were buried with your Grandad. But that would be a lie. I just wanted you back in my tummy all safe and sound.

Gradually I got back on the treadmill that is life. It was not easy but your dad and I went through the motions. It seemed that friends and family all around us were having babies. It seemed so unfair. Why did you have to be the one with the Trisomy-18? But we smiled and congratulated them and went home and cried.

Life began again for your dad and I on Saturday 28 January 1989. We could smile again without feeling sad. Your brother Ashley was born. He looked so much like you. As he grew, my heart ached for all the milestones you had missed out on. Nearly four years later we welcomed your sister Sophie into the world. What joy but also what heartache! I remember Ashley's little face when he first saw his new baby sister. I wish I could have seen your little face alongside his smiling down at her in the crib.

In trying to comfort us over the years, people have said you are our special little guardian angel up in heaven looking over us all. I do take comfort in that but sometimes I just wish you were here on earth with us sharing in those special times like birthdays and family holidays. I wish I could have kissed you better when you grazed your knee, chastised you when you walked your muddy football boots over the kitchen floor or praised you when you passed an exam or got a job. Although I am your mum I have never been your parent and that still makes me feel very sad.

I love you Nicholas and, until we meet again, God Bless.

The Ebb & Flow of a Life

1978

It began like any summer day in Southern California. The boys (eight and ten) in their summer pyjamas having breakfast and then quickly changing into swimsuits and racing to the backyard for a morning swim and game of Marco Polo. Later in the day we were at a friend's for lunch and then off to 'Mark the Barber' for their back-to-school haircuts. It was late August and school would begin in two weeks, the boys' blonde hair had grown a bit green from the chlorine in the pool and their bangs were quite overgrown in the style of the seventies Beatles.

Robbie (ten) climbed out of the barber's chair and his brother Jonathan (eight) climbed up. A few minutes into Jono's haircut, Mark asked: 'Linda, what is this in Jono's scalp?' I looked, he pointed out a thick scab maybe the size of a large pea in the crown area of Jono's scalp. I answered I didn't know but I'd get it checked out. The next day the boys and I went to our family doctor who, after examining Jono's scalp, told me he thought it was nothing. He said he imagined Jono had nicked his scalp with a comb and he wasn't concerned. I asked him to remove it anyway and he did. It was relatively quick, including a couple of stitches which would need to be removed the next week, and we went home, back to normal end of summer routine; buying new jeans, shoes, jackets, notebooks and such for the upcoming school year.

A week later we returned to the doctor's office to have Jono's two stitches removed. While in the waiting room, the nurse came to fetch me saying: 'Dr Chalek would like to see you alone.' I was thirty-one with my two children sitting in the waiting room when Conrad, Connie as our family called him, told me Jono's biopsy came back malignant. What followed was your typical nightmare: many tests at UCLA, alerting family, my parents flying in from overseas, surgery, chemo and in the end, Jonathan's death three months into fourth grade.

2000

I am driving on the freeway in Los Angeles, my three-year-old granddaughter Morgan Jade is in her car seat sitting behind me. We're playing Elmo music on the tape deck and having a delicious conversation when she says: 'Gummy, my name is Morgan Jade.' I responded: 'I know, and it's a beautiful name.' She then adds: 'Jade is for my Uncle Jonathan, he was my daddy's brother and he died. Did you know that?' I'm not sure how I controlled the steering wheel at that moment but I managed to. We talked about Jonathan and she and I drove over to the elementary school her daddy and uncle Jono had attended. I showed her the tree the fourth graders had planted in Jono's name and we sat under its strong branches.

2010

My upstate New York village is a wondrous place to live. I've been here since 2003 and I also have an apartment in Manhattan for the weeks I'm in New York City, working with a Peace Organisation affiliated with the UN. I feel like the city mouse and the country mouse, life upstate in a university town is affirming, community-minded and filled with interesting academics and their families. Time spent in New York City is exactly what you'd imagine: exciting, crowded, and stimulating. I drive between my two homes, three hundred miles apart, twice a month. The drive is a bit more than five hours and often there are friends and neighbours hitching a ride, one way or the other.

My upstate neighbours are a lovely family. I've grown very fond of them. Ezra, the dad, is a professor at the University, hair greying and a wonderful father to Agnes and little Amos. Wife and mother Charlotte is a joy. She gives me the opportunity to bake cookies with Agnes and make hummus with Amos (he likes the motor on the food processor, so we use it a lot). There are yearly handmade valentines by the children and birthday invitations, a delightful family. We often share dinners and barbecues in the yard. Ezra's father and mother live in New York City, and visit when they can. Last summer, while Ezra's father was in the village I offered to drive him back to the city at the end of the week.

The drive between the village and New York City was a great opportunity to find out more about Ezra's childhood, his brothers and their life in New York City. His dad and I had an easy and comfortable chat, including finding that politically we were much in agreement regarding big issues such as the Israeli-Palestinian conflict. But it was the smaller issues which were quite delightful, hearing his talk about his three sons, their wives and his pride in the grandchildren. As the conversation continued he said a simple sentence which began something like: 'When Ezra was born in 1969 …', I almost fainted. Once again I held on to the steering wheel and somehow managed not to drive into the oncoming traffic. Ezra was born in 1969? My greying neighbour, Agnes and Amos' daddy, the university professor, was born in 1969? And there it was, thirty-two years after Jono's death, the larger picture of what I had lost revealed itself.

2011
Today the world is trying to comprehend the triple tragedy of the 9.0 Japanese earthquake, tsunami and radiation leak. I'm trying to make sense of the ebb and flow of life and the only thing I know is we must make the most of each moment we're granted. Things change, time passes (if we're lucky) and when the golden ring on this merry-go-round called life comes by, we must grab it for we have no idea if it will ever come again. We must grab the ring knowing there is no such thing as 'forever', aware the only constant is *things change*, and our work is to find the value in each moment.

STORY WRITTEN BY ROBI DAMELIN

A Vision of Reconciliation for Israeli & Palestinian Families

I came to Israel from South Africa in 1967. I came as a volunteer after the Six Day War, thinking I'd be here for about six months. I really wanted to leave South Africa because I'd been active in the anti-apartheid movement and it was getting very pressurised and ugly. I actually wanted to live in the States. I came here and I've had this sort of love-hate relationship with this country ever since. I went to a Hebrew language programme, got married and had two kids, worked for *The Jerusalem Post*, and then with immigrants to help them find employment. After I got divorced I came to live in Tel Aviv.

I brought up my children in a very tolerant and loving, liberal way. David, Eran and I, it was kind of like a triangle – the three of us. David went to the Thelma Yellin School of the Arts because he was a very gifted musician. Out of his whole class he was probably the only one who went to the army. I was really surprised when he chose that, but I don't think you can take responsibility for somebody else's life, even if it is your child. Even in his regular army service David was torn because he didn't want to serve in the occupied territories. He became an officer and was called to go to Hebron. He was in a terrible quandary and came to me and said: 'What the hell am I going to do? I don't want to be there.' I said: 'If you want to go to jail I'll support you, but are you going to make a difference if you go to jail?' Because basically, if he were sent to jail, when he got out they'd put him somewhere else (in the occupied territories). It's a never-ending story. If it would have created a huge noise then maybe that would have been the right choice; but you can also go (to your military post) and lead by example, by treating people around you with respect.

After the army David went to Tel Aviv University and studied philosophy and psychology and then started to do his Masters in

80

Philosophy of Education. He was teaching Philosophy at a pre-military programme for potential social leaders and he was also teaching at Tel Aviv university.

Then he got called up for *miluim* and the whole issue came up again: he didn't want to go, if he goes he doesn't want to serve in the occupied territories. If he doesn't go he's letting his soldiers down? What kind of example is it for these kids who are going to be inducted into the army in two months. If he goes, he would treat anybody, any Palestinian, with respect, and so would his soldiers by his example. I said: 'Maybe you are setting a good example (by refusing to go)', and he said, 'I can't let my soldiers down, and if I don't go someone else will and will do terrible things.' I keep telling everybody that there isn't really black and white in this situation.

David went to his reserve service and I was filled with a terrible premonition, of fear I suppose. He called me on that Saturday and said: 'I have done everything to protect us. You know I love my life, but this is a terrible place, I feel like a sitting duck.' He never shared that kind of stuff with me, ever. My kids never told me what they were doing in the army. They always told me ridiculous stories, thinking that I was going to believe them. The next morning I got up very early and ran to work hours before I had to be there. I didn't want to be at home, I had a very restless feeling.

David was killed by a sniper, along with nine other people. They were at a checkpoint, a political checkpoint, near Ofra. Two days after he was killed, it was pulled down; they removed the checkpoint. I suppose all of my life I spoke about co-existence and tolerance. That must be ingrained in me because one of the first things I said is: 'You may not kill anybody in the name of my child.' I suppose that's quite unusual, an unexpected reaction to that kind of news.

It is impossible to describe what it is like to lose a child. Your whole life is totally changed forever. It's not that I'm not the same person I was. I'm the same person with a lot of pain. Wherever I go, I carry this with me. You try to run away at the beginning, but you can't. I went overseas. I went to India, I came back again, but it just goes with you wherever you go. I had a PR office and I was working with *National Geographic*, the *History Channel* and *Food & Wine* and I had all the good things in life, as well as co-existence projects with Palestinian-Israeli citizens. I wasn't particularly politically involved, it was much more on a social level: animal welfare, children, co-existence projects. I always did a lot of volunteer work; I put a lot into those kinds of things. It has always been a part of who I am. But my work began to lose all joy for me. My priorities changed completely. To sit in a meeting and decide whether a wine should be marketed in one way or another became totally irrelevant to me – I couldn't bear it. I was just very lucky, I had wonderful girls working with me in the office and they really ran the office for me for a year until I decided I couldn't bear it anymore, and I closed the office.

Yitzhak Frankenthal had come to speak to me. He was the founder of The Parents Circle – Families Forum. I wasn't sure that was the path I wanted to take, but I went to a seminar. There were a lot of Israelis and Palestinians from the group there and I didn't really feel convinced yet. But the more time went by the more I wanted to work somewhere to make a difference. It was the beginning of understanding how not to be patronising; that's a really easy trap to fall into in this kind of work: 'I know what's best for the Palestinians, let me tell them what to do.' It took me time to understand, to look at the differences in temperament, in culture, in all these things, to be much less judgemental than I'd always been. I think David was a much more tolerant person than I am, or a less judgemental person. I learned a lot of lessons from him, and the pain created a space in me that was less egocentric – that I don't know what's best for everybody.

David was killed on 3 March 2002. In October 2004 the sniper who killed David was caught, which for me was a huge step. That was really the test. 'Do I actually mean what I'm saying or am I just saying it because ... that's the test of whether I really have integrity in the work I'm doing. Do I really mean what I'm saying when I talk about reconciliation? I wrote a letter to the family. It took me about four months to make the decision, many sleepless nights and a lot of searching inside myself about whether this is what I really mean. I wrote them a letter, which two of the Palestinians from our group delivered to the family. They promised to write me a letter. It will take time; these things take time, I'm waiting. It could take five years for them to do that. They will deliver the letter that I wrote to their son who is in jail. So in my own personal development, this was the big milestone for me.

When he was caught I didn't feel anything; not satisfaction, except maybe satisfaction that he can't do it to anybody else. There is no sense of revenge and I have never looked for that.

These past years have been an incredible experience for me. I've learned so much for my own personal growth, apart from the work I'm doing, which is almost the reason I get up in the morning, actually. It's something I feel almost duty-bound to be doing; it's not a favour that I'm doing for anyone else but almost a personal mission. I know this works. I believe removing the stigma from each side and getting to know the person on the other side allows for a removal of fear, and a way to understand that a long-term reconciliation process is possible. That's also based on my background as a South African person, seeing the miracle of South Africa and how that all happened and that it was actually possible.

On David's grave there is a quotation by Khalil Gibran that says: 'The whole earth is my birthplace and all humans are my brothers.'

The Letter
This for me is one of the most difficult letters I will ever have to write. My name is Robi Damelin, I am the mother of David who was killed by your son. I know he did not kill David because he was David. If he had known him he could never have done such a thing. David was twenty-eight years old. He was a student at Tel-Aviv University doing his masters in the Philosophy of Education. David was part of the peace movement and did not want to serve in the occupied territories. He had a compassion for all people and understood the suffering of the Palestinians.

He treated all around him with dignity. David was part of the movement of the officers who did not want to serve in the occupied territories but, nevertheless, for many reasons he went to serve when he was called to the reserves.

What makes our children do what they do? They do not understand the pain they are causing your son by now having to be in jail for many years and mine who I will never be able to hold and see again or see him married, or have a grandchild from him. I can not describe to you the pain I feel since his death and the pain of his brother and girlfriend, and all who knew and loved him.

All my life I have spent working for causes of co-existence, both in South Africa and here. After David was killed I started to look for a way to prevent other families both Israeli and Palestinian from suffering this dreadful loss. I was looking for a way to stop the cycle of violence, nothing for me is more sacred than human life, no revenge or hatred can ever bring my child back. After a year, I closed my office and joined the Parents Circle – Families Forum. We are a group of Israeli and Palestinian families who have all lost an immediate family member in the conflict. We are looking for ways to create a dialogue with a long term vision of reconciliation.

After your son was captured, I spent many sleepless nights thinking about what to do: Should I ignore the whole thing, or will I be true to my integrity and to the work that I am doing and try to find a way for closure and reconciliation? This is not easy for anyone and I am just an ordinary person, not a saint. I have now come to the conclusion that I would like to try to find a way to reconcile. Maybe this is difficult for you to understand or believe, but I know that in my heart it is the only path that I can choose, for, if what I say is what I mean, it is the only way.

I understand that your son is considered a hero by many of the Palestinian people, he is considered to be a freedom fighter, fighting for justice and for an independent viable Palestinian state, but I also feel that if he understood that taking the life of another may not be the way and that if he understood the consequences of his act, he could see that a non-violent solution is the only way for both nations to live together in peace.

Our lives as two nations are so intertwined, each of us will have to give up on our dreams for the future of the children who are our responsibility.

I give this letter to people I love and trust to deliver. They will tell you of the work we are doing, and perhaps create in your hearts some hope for the future. I do not know what your reaction will be. It is a risk for me, but I believe that you will understand, as it comes from the most honest part of me. I hope that you will show the letter to your son, and that maybe in the future we can meet.

Let us put an end to the killing and look for a way through mutual understanding and empathy to live a normal life, free from violence.

- Robi's interview was edited from a long interview she gave to *Just Vision,* used here by courtesy of *Just Vision.*

CHAPTER THREE

Siblings' Stories

When you are sorrowful look again in your heart, and you shall see that in truth you are weeping for that which has been your delight.
Kahill Gibran

'Death is like a candle blowing out for the dawn to begin' is the beautiful image presented by Brian Carthy in his story, which presents a lovely transition from life to death for our siblings.

Each person copes with grief in their own way, but at the core are the precious memories of our loved ones who have left this world. In the past you may have phoned or emailed, now you just connect in a new heart and spirit level to communicate with your loved one.

The following stories of life and love and death and suffering and grieving are spoken from the hearts' of siblings. We hope you receive peace, hope and consolation in the passages of stories told by siblings whose brother or sister has died.

A Flickering Candle

From the first time I heard the expression: 'death is like a candle blowing out for the dawn to begin', it struck a chord with me. The image of a bright sunrise compared to the flickering candle for me conjures up a beautiful picture of life after death.

As a child growing up, I was well aware that, as it was put to me at the time: 'God took your sister Bridget and little brother Timothy.' I found it difficult to comprehend why God would want to come to a little remote townland in Roscommon, Ireland, and take away my brother and sister and cause my mother and father such grief and sadness. My mother often spoke to me about Bridget and Timothy when I was growing up and the loss she felt when they both died. Yet it was only in much later years, when she recounted her experiences of her children's deaths in a book about her life, that I began to fully realise the utter devastation and heartbreak she and my father had to endure.

Bridget only lived for two weeks. She had a hole in her heart. She was christened by the parish curate, Fr Tom Kilroy, at home in the kitchen of our house. My mother recalls that neighbours and friends were in the house the night Bridget died. My father was a tradesman and he made a little white coffin. It must have been utterly devastating for him to have to make a coffin for his second eldest child, but I never remember him talking about it. My mother crocheted a Christening cape with a hood, gave it to a neighbour, Bridie Egan, and said: 'Put that on Bridget, it will keep her warm.'

The following evening, a family friend, Packie Sweeney, who was an excellent flute player, played the *Coolin* soft and low before Bridget was taken from the house. I often think of the awful sadness my parents had to endure when they saw baby Bridget in the little white coffin. My mother always said that losing Bridget was like losing part of herself.

My younger brother Timothy died after just two weeks and there was more pain and heartbreak for my father and mother to endure. I visit the family grave in Lisonuffy on a regular basis and always feel peace and solace there. From the time I was a child, I was told that my brother and sister were angels in heaven and I believe that their spirit has lived on in our family.

On 4 October 2007, my older sister Rosie died while out for a stroll with her husband, Ollie, in Strokestown. Little did any of us know when Rosie came home to Ireland for a short holiday that it would be the final journey back to the place of her birth – the little townland at the foothills of Sliabh Bán that shaped her life and prepared her for the road ahead.

None of us could have known that her time had come. Rosie herself though, had a special affinity with God. I always felt that she was in touch with God in a way that was beyond our under-standing. Rosie always had a devotion to St Francis of Assisi and how extraordinary it was that she died so suddenly on his feast day, 4 October.

Indeed, Rosie had told some family and friends on the day before she died that she had the 'Golden Key'. Even though Rosie's health had been poor for some time, her death was totally unex-pected.

Rosie liked nothing better than to come home on holidays to visit Mother. Clearly, mother and daughter had a special bond and it must have been preordained by a greater power that Rosie be at home in Ireland when she passed away so suddenly. We are so appreciative that so many came to her assistance in her final moments as she herself gave much of her own life to the nursing profession, where she brought comfort, healing and hope to so many.

Through my work as a Gaelic Games Correspondent and commentator with RTÉ Radio Sport, I have attended many sad funerals. It is particularly devastating when a young person dies. I am always struck by the strong faith of those grieving, despite having to cope with devastatingly sad circumstances. Everyone has their own way of coping with grief but at the centre of it all are the precious memories of those who have lived among us but are now enjoying a new dawn. I have always believed that the spirit of those we knew and loved on this earth will remain with us always.

STORY WRITTEN BY KYLA BONNSTETTER

Beautiful & Free At Last

It was six o'clock in the morning. The phone never rings at that hour, so I knew something was terribly wrong. It was my mother, and I could barely make out her words. She was crying, and didn't have to speak. I already knew. My sister wasn't coming out of this one. She was suffering from, what doctor's called, a permanent vegetative state. It was her time. I was on my way.

It must have been the longest drive of my life and, to make things worse, I missed my exit. I was crying hysterically. Maybe I didn't want to face the inevitable. Because, how do you say goodbye? How do you watch your only sister, your best friend and confidante, slowly die? While we witnessed so many answered prayers over the years, the days of praying for just one more miracle were over.

Saibra was two-and-a-half years younger than me, but she was my big sister and my protector every time I needed her. I admired her and looked up to her and always asked her for advice that she so freely gave. She was honest and would tell you exactly what she thought, never holding back. She would do anything for me. While Saibra never had children of her own, she took great pride in being an Aunt to my son. She loved him as her own.

In high school, Saibra took the star role in every play. She was a singer, a cheerleader, a writer – just your all around over-achiever. We were complete opposites, but we were best friends. Growing up, all we had was each other. To this day, Saibra is the only person who 'gets' me and my sense of humour. Our endless 'inside' jokes which were only hilarious to us – and almost always directed at our mother, a single mom who did her best – are what I'll miss the most.

Saibra was ailing for many years. This I knew. Still, I couldn't wrap my head around what was happening. Deep down inside, I thought she'd be okay, she'd recover. She had to! She was my sister, my best friend, my Baa Baa – one of the many endearing nicknames I had for her.

But, this time her illness would overtake her. An earlier DNA test revealed cystic fibrosis of the digestive system. She was fighting it, but it led to many complications – diabetes and a rare pancreatic condition. It was simply too much for her frail body to handle any more.

At the young age of forty-one, Saibra had lost her battle and her life. She was in and out of the hospital most of her life, and in a coma for her last five months. She died on 18 October 2010. It was a Monday.

When I walked into her room, I found my mother crying next to my sister's body. My heart physically ached. Through puffy, tear-soaked eyes, I saw something that took me by surprise. My sister looked beautiful. She looked peaceful. And, for the first time in years, she appeared pain-free. Saibra's delicate, porcelain face appeared calm, soothing, angelic. She had suffered so much, for so long. Finally, she was free. I find peace in knowing her suffering had finally ended. She was free at last. God set her free.

We sat next to my sister's bedside, next to her body, for almost six hours. This was surreal. It was comforting and comfortable to be with her body. It brought a little closure, if ever there could be. I remember my mom saying, 'What do we do now?' Neither one of us had an answer, and it was okay.

Her funeral was lovely, a true celebration of Saibra's life and the wonderful impact she had on us all. It made me realise how special life is – that life is a gift many of us take for granted. I have found great comfort in getting to know her friends on a deeper level as we grieve and support each other.

Even in death, Saibra's guiding me and teaching me, the way she had in life. You never know the last time you're going to see someone. And, many of us never realise the significance of our personal interactions, until it is your last. Thanks to my sister, and the lessons she's taught me, I now strive to make every moment count.

Saibra's Memorial Programme

I'm Free
Don't grieve for me, for now I'm free
I'm following the path God laid for me.
I took his hand when I heard him call;
I turned my back and left it all.
I could not stay another day,
To laugh, to love, to work or play.
Tasks left undone must stay that way;
I found that place at the close of day.
If my parting has left a void,
Then fill it with remembered joy.
A friendship shared a laugh, a kiss;
Ah yes, these things, I too will miss.
Be not burdened with times of sorrow,
I wish you the sunshine of tomorrow.
My life's been full, I savoured much;
Good friends, good times, a loved ones' touch.
Perhaps my time seems all too brief
Don't lengthen it now with undue grief.
Lift up your heart and share with me:
'God wanted me now, He set me free.'
Author unknown

Suicide to a Sibling

The last few hours, or weeks, or months, maybe it was years. A plan was in place in my mind.

I knew that somehow it would come to this, that's what gave me the energy and confidence to go through with it.

A gun, one of three I owned, well, because I could own one and no questions were asked.

I remember visiting at a friend's house, his dad was a colonel in the Irish army and he came home in full uniform with a pistol in its holster attached to his belt. The gun scared me so much that my mother had to come and console me and eventually take me home. Irrational really but my first experience ... fear of what was to come?

I wasn't always packing but I knew what was about to happen when I got the phone call from my clients. Their dream home was a disaster. This was the final straw – the last stand.

This was my destiny and nothing anyone could say or do could have deterred me from this action. Not my wife, son or daughter, mother or father could have offered a reprieve. No it was final and over.

It was my total fixation now.

Suicidal thoughts were not a regular part of my life at all. I was down, I suppose depressive, unable to get sleep without alcohol and then only getting a few hours.

I know what people thought when I passed. I was able to gain insights in spirit. There was anger, frustration and guilt. There was love and pity. None of it caused me to wish I could undo the ending.

I return all the emotions with love

This love eventually allowed those who wished me back to be still. It is OK that I passed by my own hand. Much of their passion in this regard was to do with themselves and deep memories and feelings that my death allowed to surface; the same as with all bereavements. The pain never goes – one just gets accustomed to living with it.

The life here was great, fast-paced and always with new experiences available. I loved speed and nothing better than taking the bike out and pushing it to the limit of the road, it's engineering and my ability. Often past my ability – that was the rush when I was alone but with an audience I wanted to stand out and make them aware of my presence and power.

Building houses gave me enormous satisfaction at the start. I was with guys that I loved, not necessarily the individuals but the competitive nature of any group of men, some with interests I shared, some with skills I admired but mainly I was the leader of this 'pack'.

It was a good business and making money was not a problem, perhaps it came too easily because when the errors in judgement started to become more frequent – well I think that they were because of my inexperience – going too fast, running before I could walk.

I had loads of friends, my nature was to befriend people if I liked them. My way was instant reaction: 'I like you so cut the bullshit and behave like we have a long standing bond and loyalty to one another. Let's know each other in a few hours.'

Brian's Story
Fergus was my first grieving. I felt that the edge from the loss of Fergus was dulled by his being away for so long, he was not immediate. Secondly my own family, Susan my wife especially, gave me support and a sense of grounding that gave grieving a space without dominating.

I allowed the grief to come and it visited frequently. Our funeral process was a day of wailing and visits to my parents' house of lots of friends and relatives. Then seeing off those who were going to travel to America, then emptiness and support.

We gathered in the priest's home in Newbridge to participate in the Funeral Mass which was going on in Portland, MA. We listened on the phone to the eulogy. The grief experienced was a variety of emotions and reactions. Tears would come like a dam bursting. Sometimes I could cry silently, other times the sobbing was attracting attention, but I let it happen, or at least did nothing to curtail or stop it. It was a rolling ride. I would have normality, dealing with the world and being completely rational then

94

the feeling might just erupt. Sometimes a cry was very welcome and it cleared a space for me.

I often tried to understand why I was grieving. Was it for my own loss? Was it for Fergus himself, now cold and no more? Was it for his wife Holly? His daughter Caitlín or son Tadhg? It was sometimes for all of them; sometimes for none. I was surrounded by people who were reflecting their own experience of the loss of a loved one and the emotions were in due course projected.

I had been told sometime that in some Islam cultures it is believed that at birth God gave each soul a certain number of breaths. This was a paradigm that I held onto when Fergus died. It meant to me that Fergus, while he controlled what he did while here, had no control on when he would go. No matter how it happened, he would 'exit' at that exact breath. That being the case, then his existence led him to the point that he would take his own life.

We often see headlines where a person was killed in a single car accident. It is not beyond my own belief that many of these deaths are suicidal. This is not intended to cause, to the loved ones of those who have died in this manner, upset but just to raise awareness of the possibility of it being the correct version of events. On the other side of the equation is the occasion where a person intent on self-destruction will also take out others, almost in the mode of al-Qaeda. This perspective is purely as an insight from my rationalisations during my grieving. I know it is unkind and perhaps insensitive to those who have lost loved ones in traffic accidents and I am aware that a parent, brother or child does not need to have to deal with the idea that others died in the suicide of their cherished one.

Where did he go? Religious beliefs allow us little conjecture on this question. My own spiritual understanding is that Fergus has passed on, no longer an entity in this realm but completely alive and vital in another. When I wanted to communicate with Fergus previously I would phone or write a card (prior to email). I am now comfortable sending what can best be described as mental messages to him. The difference now is that I don't expect a response in real time or even in real terms – maybe no response at all. In fact I have no expectations whatsoever – the peace and calm of sending my messages to Fergus is an immediate benefit and satisfies my need.

What did Fergus leave behind?
His beautiful, strong and focused daughter, Caitlín, from his first marriage to Kim. Caitlín was put into a massive spin, first to lose her Dad from the home, then to lose him completely from her life. As a pre-teen, with support from those people who loved her, Caitlín has moved on in her life as only a young person can. I know that Caitlín has achieved to her full ability and I have no doubt she will make a full contribution to society perhaps in spite of the tragedy of losing her father to suicide.

Tadhg was perhaps too young to fully understand what happened apart from the reality that his father, the strong male influence was gone from his life. Certainly he was too young to be able to express in a meaningful way his feelings about all that had happened. I have no honest opinion on how Tadhg's life will evolve, but of course the tragedy will have a strong influence on him for better or worse.

Justin lived in Portland and was a constant in Fergus's life and *vice versa*. There is no describing the depth of despair that must have descended into his life when he received the news that Fergus had died.

An interesting point is the reaction to the news of a death. My experience with Fergus was mixed in that the first thoughts were about the issues of death, the finality and end of life. These were quickly followed by the suicide – why, what was he thinking, could I have done anything? These two concepts – the death and the cause of death – soon became rolled into one. I soon realised that they need to be thought of as separate, especially in this instance (suicide) and in other tragic and sudden deaths.

My brothers, sister and parents decided that we would be completely open with regard to Fergus's death. We were quite clear to any inquisitor that he ended his own life. To protect the innocent we did not necessarily describe in detail the final moments and how he ended his life, although I did want to shock a certain person who seemed to be taking a voyeuristic approach to offering me condolences.

I believe that this approach gave many people the opportunity to revisit their own experiences around suicide. Perhaps empowering them to ask questions and I hope that it allowed many to take a similar stance when they were faced with a similar situation.

Suicide is a legitimate cause of death. By this I mean that, in older times, suicide was a 'hidden' cause of death so as to save the honour of the dead person or save the family left behind from the stigma and ensure burial in consecrated ground. Nowadays the media will report on a suicide mostly in a matter of fact way, which further helps to remove the stigma.

Does this mean that a potential victim could find it easier to consider taking their own life because of the lesser gravity of the act on those left behind? I don't believe that a person thinking of suicide would be considering such an argument in their contemplation.

Story written by Helen Jackson

At Peace & Rest: Our Messengers of Love

I had a lovely brother Dilly until November 2005 when he sadly passed away. He was only fifty-eight years old. He had a heart disease from the age of twenty-three so was regularly in and out of hospital having various operations. But each time he would bounce back from death's door to fight another day and have another pint. So his passing was a great shock to all my family. Luckily, in one way, at this time my mother was suffering from Alzheimer's disease and was in a local nursing home. She had previously shared the home place with Dilly and he had cared for her for some years. Therefore, she did not have to experience the painful grief as she was very confused at that time. She also died five months after Dilly's death, so they sort of went together in my mind and that in itself was comforting at the time. As it happens our immediate family had not had a death for over thirty years previously, so within the space of one year I was an orphan and life within the home place had changed dramatically. I was shocked at how much the deaths affected me, especially my brother's. I took it for granted that he would always be there.

He had always made it before. I slept badly, smoked more and more, did not eat, felt such a great loss; I cried and cried for days. As a district nurse and in between visiting my own patients I sobbed and sobbed. Then I attended my patients cheerfully enough. I felt I couldn't get a handle on this at all. That's me, with over thirty years nursing experience under my belt. I nursed many terminal patients and advised families how to cope, etc. But when it's your own family, nurse or doctor, I think your career is of no help at all.

I dreadfully missed hearing his voice on the phone at times. Having left the siblings in Ireland I felt cut off for the first time ever. My other brother in the USA had difficulty coping so I spent a lot of my evenings comforting him on the phone. I think with not having had children myself, my siblings were the most important people in my life.

My husband was somehow separate from this in my mind, as if he could not possibly know or share my childhood memories with my big brother. But how could he? He has always been the most loving and supportive husband, luckily for me. It was like something I could not control and nothing could change it back to how it used to be.

All the tears in the world can't change it or make it better. Even though I know that he was weary of this condition and its limitations on his activities, it never made a bit of difference to the overwhelming feelings of grief that I felt. Then I began to wonder was I holding on to this grief for me, as in fear of letting go. I had read all the books and taken all the courses to do with loss. Why was I finding it so hard to let go? I knew I should let go but I didn't know how. I so wanted to be able to manage my thinking and channel it appropriately at this time which unconsciously I must have done to have continued working full-time as I did. But I kept returning in my mind to his body laid out and felt the pain each time. As if I needed to keep that alive in my head and let the cortisone flow around to fan the fire. What for? To keep him with us? Perhaps it's the Catholic in me having to sacrifice and suffer the pain again and again?

I woke up one night crying, as I had dreamt that Dilly did not know he was dead and had just found out. He cried and cried. It was so very real and he was standing there crying with his big white handkerchief wet through. I had a panic that night as I couldn't remember what colour his eyes were. I played a lot of music late at night at that time. That was maybe six months after his death. Funnily enough after that dream I felt that he was at peace and slowly I began to recover a little day by day in the knowledge that he was settled and OK and I felt a real feeling of knowing *that* for sure. I cannot believe to this day the enormity of the loss I felt and still feel at times. I can't begin to understand how it feels to lose a spouse or child. I just block that out and hope I will never have to deal with it.

My mother's death is as though it's in a different category, one of old age and time to die, as it should be. I miss her dreadfully at times but find myself smiling when I think of her, which is every day, of the things she said and did. I had a super mother and sadly Alzheimer's disease prepared us by stealing her slowly a little at a time until her mind was gone but still she loved to see the new day, so she lives on in every new day. With Dilly I still want the photo to talk back but not so desperately nowadays. It has helped me to feel more empathy for others and to live life for the now as they would want me to.

You know, I do believe all these feelings of loss are absolutely normal/necessary to the grieving process. But I still say that for me *time* has helped and continues to do so. Nature, which can be so cruel at times, I feel, does protect one. I have just attended a family gathering and for the first time I didn't expect both of them to show up, but that has been five years and a few visits there. The family dynamics continue to change with weddings and births which is, of course, great cause for celebration.

The Little-One's Story

My brother Paddy Joe was the oldest in the family so I always looked up to him as a big brother. As youngsters our pastime was out in the field kicking a football around and hurling and he always had to be in charge.

There is a time that stands out in my mind. He was sent to pick up a load of bonhams (young pigs) and, of course, I wanted to go along. He insisted it was too cold and refused to take me, so I cried and cried until my mother stepped in and told him to take me, but he was not happy. That was one of the many ways he wanted to protect me.

He was always great at telling old stories and yarns. We would sit up half the night listening to him. That was a big part of his personality.

At the age of seventy-five years, he was diagnosed with advanced prostate cancer.

For twelve months he underwent all radiation and chemotherapy treatments to no avail, and in the end he succumbed to that dreadful illness. He passed away in his own home surrounded by his family and friends. He passed away peacefully.

I miss his presence everywhere. What keeps me going is knowing he is no longer in pain and I know he is with God. The memories will always be cherished. My family and good friends are a tremendous support. Due to my busy workload, he is greatly missed and I turn to him in prayer to help me get through it.

I have learned to deal with my loss by keeping busy and surrounding myself with my friends and never turning down an invitation to get out of the house. I get great solace in talking to him through prayer. A little advice to people who are grieving – try your best to keep busy.

CHAPTER FOUR

Friends' Stories

While we are mourning the loss of our friend,
others are rejoicing to meet him behind the veil.
John Taylor

Pain has a way of clipping our wings and keeping us from being able to fly,
and if left unresolved for very long, you can almost forget that you were ever
created to fly in the first place.
William P Young (The Shack)

This quotation is a reminder to us to carry on,
though the loss severe.

Tim Maloney reminds us in *The Redemption Tree* that loss, grief
and grieving are hard concepts to explain. He poses the following questions: When does grief end? Where does grief go? What
fills the void left by grief? These are challenging questions for
each person to reflect on as you journey on the grieving road of
life. Perhaps all of life is a letting-go of some sort or other. We let
go of school, career, business, friends and family on our journey
and quest for destiny - perhaps.

We thank God for the presence of our friends in our lives and
their understanding and giftedness and we cherish the
memories of our love shared.

The following stories of life and love and death and suffering
and grieving are spoken from the hearts' of friends and colleagues. We hope you receive peace, hope and consolation in the
passages of stories told by friends and colleagues
whose loved one has died.

Enjoy Life & Live in the Present Moment

I first met John Butler in 2006. The context of our discussion was a programme John had developed called *Odyssey: The Business of Consulting*. It was a real draw for me. I had a vision of where I wanted to go and I had been searching for a solid strategy to take me to the next level. Until I talked with John, I had no clearly defined strategy to achieve that.

When the five-day Odyssey session was offered in January 2007, I was there with four other consultants. I worked through the experience with John and Imelda Butler, and Rolando Marchis, and I got to know them as friends.

My friend John was a man of faith, a committed husband and proud father, a good family man. He was a man of action. High energy. Intelligent. Thoughtful. Creative. Fun. Visionary. Action-oriented. Kind. Direct. Positive. Realistic. Entertaining. Committed. Values-driven.

Chuck Swindoll, in his character sketch and study of King David, identifies four levels of friendship: acquaintances, casual friends, close friends, and intimate friends. Swindoll defines intimate friends as 'those few people with whom we have regular contact and a deep commitment. We are not only open and vulnerable with these people, we anxiously await their counsel. Intimate friends are just as free to criticise and to correct us as they are to embrace and encourage, because trust and mutual understanding has been established between them.'

The kind of friendship that King David and his friend Jonathan enjoyed was a level four friendship … the kind of friendship I enjoyed with John.

One thing that took our friendship to level four was a project we took on in 2010, co-authoring a book on the theme: 'Is Your Business Model Right for These Times?'

We set the goal on 12 May to complete the book by 1 August. We worked very closely and were in frequent contact by phone and email.

By 23 July, a Friday, we had the book 85% completed, with significant work yet to be done. That day, we had a Skype conference call with the publisher to brainstorm and finalise the title of the book (*Business Model Innovation: Proven Strategies That Actually Work*).

On that Skype conference call, we kept getting cut off from the publisher. John and I would wait until we could reconnect. It gave us a chance to talk one-to-one about the direction of our three-way conversation. At one point, John gently nudged me in an interlude by saying: 'Let's stay in the present moment, and see how this conversation develops – I really like where he is going.' This was so like John, deftly making a point to achieve better results in a 'master practitioner' communications moment.

The 'present moment awareness' concept which John often highlighted is exactly as it suggests: staying very alert to all that is going on right now, absorbing and processing it while resisting the urge to race ahead to what's next. This principle is very important in building solid relationships with business owners and executives.

To achieve our aggressive goal of completing the book in a ten-week timeframe, John and Imelda were often up in the early morning, 4 or 5 a.m., to get their part done. They were up very early on that Saturday, 24 July to review the latest edits I'd sent them. They both felt very good about where the book was heading with the latest copy and edits.

John and I had an appointment to talk early on Monday, 26 July to complete the book before the holidays during the first two weeks of August. Before I left for work that Monday morning, I was reading the book I mentioned earlier (Charles Swindoll, *David: A Man of Passion and Destiny*). The principle that stuck with me that day was that one of God's gifts to us is that he does not let us know what is in the future. This was an interesting reminder to enjoy our present moment, tying in with the conversation I'd had with John on Friday.

I called John at our appointed time that Monday morning. No answer. Stranger yet, no e-mail from John that day … it was totally unlike him. I took the call from Rolando that afternoon to let me know that John had passed away on Sunday. I was shocked. I've lost friends and family to death before ... but I've never felt the blow of death to that extent. It was totally unexpected. Our collaboration had been so intense to achieve the goal of completing our book by 1 August. Our friendship was very close, our camaraderie was unique, our shared values and personal bond were deep.

Truly, not knowing the future is one of God's remarkable gifts to us. Had I known the future when I was talking with John on 23 July, it would have been a miserable moment for me. I could not have enjoyed the time we had that day.

As I think back to that last conversation I had with John, and his encouragement for me to stay in the present moment, I am reminded of the lyrics of the song by Bill and Gloria Gaither, *We Have This Moment, Today.*

I have a lot of rich memories of time spent with my very good friend John, time that then was 'today' – the present moment. And that is a life lesson I'll never forget: live life with a healthy focus on the here and now, in the present.

I'm reminded of the words of Winston Churchill: 'It is a mistake to look too far ahead. Only one link of the chain of destiny can be handled at a time.'

The Redemption Tree

Loss, grief and grieving are hard concepts to explain to oneself. What do good outcomes to a grieving process look like? When does grief end? Where does it go? If grief is that emptiness and sense of a void within us, in the end what fills in that void when we have dealt with it? What replaces grief in our mindset and inner being?

One day I came across this strange looking tree on my route to work and pulled over to look at it. It had at one time surely been one of those majestic looking Maple trees which we have all over this part of the world, which are somewhat taken for granted. I imagined that it had absorbed some fairly traumatic damage during its life from disease, lightening strikes etc. It now had a somewhat less than stately appearance, but the stories it could tell, if able.

Once I found its location, over the following three-four year period I would make sure that I checked on it. I wanted this tree to last forever. Somehow it spoke to me in a way that nothing else did. Enduring, courageous and stoic were adjectives that came to mind when I thought of it.

I continued to drive past it in those years always marvelling at its ability to create beauty under some very trying circumstances until one day I arrived to find that the inevitable had finally caught up with the tree and it had been cut down and the area around it bulldozed to make way for progress and yet another building development.

One day a friend sent me a card and on it was a picture that he had taken of my tree. Coincidentally he had seen it too. He had come through tough business situations and considered the tree to be his rallying symbol; he called it his Redemption Tree.

I have kept the tree picture in my desk drawer and pull it out to look at it from time to time and think of what it was saying to me.

Redemption: the act of deliverance from something that allows us to feel complete and back to normal, or in homeostasis.

The principle of homeostasis is that a living organism is either growing or dying, there is no real *status quo*, no standing still. We are either creating or we are not.

While our physical vehicle may wear out on us through age, illness or catastrophic cause like an accident, our mind, what it creates for us and what we leave in others minds, is our true purpose. Clarity and purpose are found through others and only then revealed to ourselves.

How do we explain the unexplainable?

I have a friend John who passed away leaving much too early. He left much too early for me, his friends and his family. However, what he left behind through his thoughts, writing and guidance to others somehow more than balances out the fact that he did leave us.

His voice is still heard everyday through what was and who he left behind. Would we have liked even more? Is there a conversation or undone act that we now wish we had? Of course, however, what he did share was enough. How many of us can say we did enough?

Is John missed? Yes. Did he do his share on behalf of his purpose to himself and others? The answer rings out as an even more resounding ... Yes!

I had a near-death experience. My own health issue was with a rare blood cancer in the form of an acute leukaemia.

The grief that I now understand better than most is more, 'What if ...?' than, 'What happened?' I didn't deserve what I got and it has been my observation since that very few people do.

Further into my thoughts I realised that while I had achieved some good things and created a good life for myself and my family, I questioned whether I had done enough to leave my mark on the broader world? Would the legacy of my existence here be carried on through others?

My personal satisfaction index wasn't reading 'mission accomplished'.

This maple tree picture now represents something different to me. One can be battered by many of life's circumstances like job loss, relationship problems, financial concerns, catastrophic health issues and finally death itself. Seemingly, in all but the last case, there is a chance to be redeemed, to come through our challenge.

In the case of death that redemption comes through what we leave others to carry forward. Our thoughts and guidance to others, becomes integral. Depending on circumstances and an unexpected early departure from life, a financial legacy might be impossible. However, like my friend John the philanthropy of self is open to us all.

We have models of possibility like John in front of us daily.

For me to be lucky enough to have come out the other side from what I faced is something to reflect back to but I can't live there. I have been one of the fortunate few who received a second chance at legacy. The length of that chance in terms of time is unknown.

I will be vital again. Physically, I might never be the tree I was. I can still be good. My opportunity to contribute ideas, thinking and a point of view is once again available.

Perhaps that is what happens to grief when we have accepted its message?

Death ends a life, not a relationship

Martin was a larger than life character, no mean feat considering he stood at five feet six inches, and he was generous in every respect. I first encountered him at a parish council meeting, and discovered that he was a governor of my children's school, as well as holding various other voluntary posts. Very soon I learned that Martin was a devout Catholic, a devoted husband to Hilary and a loving father and grandfather. Nothing too remarkable you might be thinking. However, on 17 March every year, Martin's Irish roots came to the fore at the annual event he hosted to celebrate St Patrick's Day. Think of a real life-size leprechaun and that is what Martin turned into, much to the amusement of all who knew him in Essex. The event also gave Martin, in his own mind at least, a forgivable excuse for breaking his Lenten abstinence from drink. Subsequent to St Patrick's Day, the excuses would follow thick and fast. For instance, attendance at any Six Nations match would be deemed to be a pilgrimage and another excuse for freedom from his abstinence.

Martin's natural charm and wonderful sense of humour was loved by all age groups. Martin would always be one of those you could rely on to support any good cause and, at a quiz night I organised, my fifteen-year-old daughter and twenty-three-year old niece joined Martin and his group of fellow OAPs on their table. The girls were still talking and laughing at 4.00 a.m. about the banter and wonderful night they had in Martin's company. Martin was a practical joker to all he knew. However, on at least one occasion I saw his 'victims' get their own back.

I once commented on a lovely photo of Hilary and Martin where they both looked extremely happy. He was quick to fill me in on the reason for their joy. The photo was taken at Newark Airport. Hilary was happy because she was returning on the planned date and Martin was delighted to be able to delay his return, thus allowing him to remain in USA to see more of Ireland competing in the 1994 World Cup.

On 7 August 2003, Martin was sadly diagnosed with Motor Neurone Disease (MND). MND is a progressive neuro-degenerative disease that attacks the upper and lower motor neurones. Degeneration of the motor neurones leads to weakness and wasting of muscles, causing increasing loss of mobility in the limbs and difficulties with speech, swallowing and breathing. I knew what a cruel disease this is and, as a friend, I hoped that Martin would be spared his speech being affected, maybe selfishly on my part, because I just knew it was his banter that I loved.

When people would say 'We will pray for a miracle,' Martin's unselfish response was to say, 'Leave the miracles for the young.' One of his only wishes was to make it to his seventy-fifth birthday. Martin passed away on the morning of his seventy-fifth birthday. Martin's philosophy throughout his illness was never to say: 'Why me?' but rather, 'Why not me?' From the time of Martin's diagnosis, his outlook seemed to be to make it easier for all around him to deal with it. He once said: 'It is not me that suffers with MND, it is my family.'

MND can often be difficult to diagnose. Martin's GP, (another of his female admirers! You knew them all Hilary!) regularly asked Martin to come into the surgery to allow medical students to question him as part of their training. This was a typically selfless act on Martin's part, especially as the progression of the disease was hindering his mobility. This same GP who is a thorough professional, was to break down in tears on his doorstep on the Monday morning, following his death on the Saturday, such was his impact on all he met. She was calling on her way into work, to see how he had been over the weekend. She had not heard the sad news that Martin had passed away on the Saturday morning.

As anyone who has cared twenty-four-seven for somebody, and as Hilary would confirm, one of the huge walls you hit along the way is when you just can't get them to eat. As the disease progressed, Martin's ability to swallow deteriorated. During this time, Hilary mashed, blended and liquidised the food but her love for Martin remained solid. Swallowing food continued to be a problem over the last few months as the disease progressed. As a carer you feel once you can't provide food that the person can find appetising and manage to swallow you are failing and the one thing you thought you could do is not working. It is then that reality hits home, that they are not getting better.

On the morning of 16 February 2008, I was dropping my daughter to her Saturday job and was intending to visit Martin. On the way I received a phone call from Hilary. Once I heard her voice I just said: 'I am on my way', she proceeded to tell me in her gentle way that I was too late.

When I arrived a few minutes later on the morning of Martin's seventy-fifth birthday, I felt there was a peace and calm. Martin looked at peace. His suffering was over. At the house was his dear friend of over forty years, our retired parish priest. How would this affect him, losing a trustworthy, loyal and fun friend?

On the eve of Martin's seventy-fifth birthday, Hilary spent time preparing food for the family who would be visiting the next day, while Martin watched television in the lounge. She regrets this and felt she should have been sitting beside Martin had she been able to foresee the events of the next twenty-four hours.

What made him have such an impact on me and so many others? The glint in his eye, the relentless humour, the common sense, the ability to relish life irrespective of what it throws at you, the banter and the craic. The fact that he played such an important part voluntarily in the work of the school where my two children received the best possible start to their education, the constant behind the scenes support and so many other things made Martin special to me, but the main thing was that Martin was Martin. He was the good guy with the good fun all rolled into one.

Has Martin left a legacy? Most certainly. Hilary could never understand sport, or was it Martin's obsession she couldn't understand? Now, during the Six Nations if you want an analysis of any game no better person to ask than Hilary! Her children look in amazement when she can reel off football results and give her thoughts on Roy Keane's departure from Ipswich. I just feel that it is Martin carrying on doing the impossible, still bringing a smile to many a face. Hilary continues to fundraise for the

MND society and these events are always supported by a large group of their friends. Martin, I would say, left a positive mark on all who met him. The vast majority of us would just like a little of what he had, or at least to learn a little from his human touch.

As a friend do I have regrets? Of course I do: I should have visited more, I should have questioned more and learnt more from this great human being. This, however, would have changed the dynamics of our friendship. Also, had I done these things, at the time, it may have been intrusive. Would I wish Martin back? To talk to, most certainly, but not for one second to go through what he did with this cruel disease. So I have to surmise that I was extremely lucky to have met one of the best and to hopefully be able to learn from his great philosophy on dealing with the adversities that life can throw at you.

Mary Ann, At Peace with Death

I met Mary Ann in the fall of 2009. We were thrown together at a church renewal retreat weekend with twenty other women who would be known as Christ Renews His Parish (CRHP) Team 8. Over the next six months, we met weekly as a group to share our pasts, our faith, and our love of God.

CRHP Team 8 was a mixed bag of nuts. We were young and old ranging in age from late 20s to early 80s. We were married, single, divorced, and widowed. We were working, unemployed, self-employed and retired. We came for friendship, answers, purpose, healing and love.

Mary Ann and I were very different and we didn't really like each other at first. I was too rigid for her taste and she was too loud and obnoxious for mine. She had the cropped hair cut of one who is recovering from chemotherapy. I didn't know her story at first and was afraid to ask. But as each week would come and go, I would learn about Mary Ann's history and what brought her to this place.

In January, 2009, after too many years of smoking too many cigarettes, Mary Ann was diagnosed with an aggressive inoperable form of lung cancer. While her prognosis was not good – without treatment she would live 2 months and with treatment she might have 2 years give or take – her faith in God was worse.

She started receiving prescribed medical treatments and at the same time with the support of her loving family she began to seek God's healing love. In addition to weekly chemo and radiation, she would attend Mass every week. The treatments caused her to lose hair, weight and hope. But the prayer and encouragement of family and friends helped her go on. After only 6 weeks, she was ready to die. But her family encouraged her to continue, so she did. Until she finally asked God, 'Please give me the strength to continue with the treatments or the strength to stop.'

When I met Mary Ann, she had stopped all treatment and was waiting to die. I wasn't sure that I wanted to be part of her journey. I was afraid of investing myself emotionally in some-one who would not be around in another six months. But the Holy Spirit was working in CRHP Team 8 and, like it or not, Mary Ann and I became friends.

The CRHP process opened Mary Ann's eyes and heart even more to God. One Monday evening, as we were gathering for our weekly meeting, Mary Ann announced to the team that she had been reading the Bible and couldn't put it down. 'There's a lot of good stuff in there!' she exclaimed. It was a blessing for me to witness God's work in her life as He revealed Himself to her. The 'peace of God that surpasses all understanding' (Phil 4:7) was surely reflected in Mary Ann's life. She prayed more than ever before. We all did.

Mary Ann made the commitment to participate in the next women's CRHP weekend in six months, but her biggest fear was that she would not be well enough to make it through the process. When she started feeling familiar pains in her side, she decided to go back to the doctors. It was the end of January 2010. A week later, the PET (Positron emission tomography) scan re-vealed that the cancer was gone.

What? Gone? Are you sure? No more cancer? What was she going to do now?

Mary Ann had spent a year preparing for her death and she was at peace with it. Now, it was the prospect of life that was just as unsettling as the original cancer diagnosis. What was she going to do with her life? The first answer was the easy one for someone who was as loud and obnoxious as she. She threw a party – a big rebirthing party! It was a wonderful celebration of the miracle of life.

She went back to work and continued with CRHP Team 8 as we prepared for the upcoming renewal weekend. She knew that God had plans for her. Her openness to His love and willingness to do His will was an inspiration to me. For this reason, I suggest-ed that she might consider starting a cancer ministry at our church to help others who would travel the same path. She liked the idea, but had other more pressing things to address, so the idea just sat there.

The more pressing things, it turned out, was a large tumour that had developed on her brain. She began suffering from dizziness, blurred vision and erratic blood pressure. Thinking that she might be having a stroke, she was rushed to the hospital. After a series of tests, it was determined that the cancer that we thought was gone had moved to her brain. The prognosis: six months.

After a good, strong cry, I went to visit Mary Ann that evening. She was out on the lanai, smoking a cigarette – never did give the darn things up - and laughter filled the air. Two other CRHP Team 8 members were there and jokes were flying. There was an odd sense of merriment. It was odd to me, but not odd to Mary Ann.

She was not dying. She was living. Each day was a blessing from God and she realized that even with this tumour in her head, God had a purpose for her life and each day He gave her, she gave back to Him.

Over the next few months, I visited her often. We'd sit and talk about whatever was on her mind that day. Sometimes she would tell me about what she had planned. Other times she'd talk about her visions - the little boy up in the treehouse who was visible only to her. She often would ask me to do a favour. Sometimes it was small, like bringing her favourite chocolate pie which I would have to hide so the rest of her family wouldn't eat it. Sometimes it was big, like having a lullaby she sang to her grandchildren put to music and recorded on a CD. Regardless of the size of the request, I was always given a big, toothy smile in return and she never let me leave without first saying 'I love you'.

Mary Ann started to fail quickly. She would tire easily and seizures came more frequently. Each time, her family would move into action as they had been trained by the hospice nurses. Everyone knew the end was near and we all prayed she would pass peacefully - everyone except Nanny, Mary Ann's mom. She held on to the hope that there would be another miracle.

I had one last, and very special, visit with a conscious Mary Ann. She was smoking non-stop but could not see well enough to light the cigarette nor could she hold it in her hand. So disregarding my personal dislike for smoking, I patiently lit and held them for her, one after another, trying to avoid the second-hand smoke. She knew how much I hated her smoking so in gratitude, she offered me a bite of her favorite chocolate pie - holding the fork for me. It was sweet.

There were two more visits by her bedside. I quietly sat and prayed the rosary. Nanny finally accepted the inevitable and told Mary Ann she could go. Mary Ann died the next day. It was the first time I cried since I heard about her second diagnosis. But this time, the tears were more joyful than before. I knew Mary Ann had gone to the place Jesus had prepared for her and she was ready to go.

Mary Ann lived an amazing seven months after receiving her second death notice. She was able to put her life in order so her family could be at peace when she was gone. She was able to witness her grandchildren receive their First Holy Communion – something she was committed to make happen. She took her first trip to Walt Disney World which included riding as the Grand Marshall in the parade. She went on a cruise. She watched the butterflies. She had non-stop visits from her friends and she saw angels. She was given the opportunity to say 'goodbye' and 'I love you' to her family and friends.

One year to the day after her 'rebirthing' party, another party was held to launch 'Hope is Contagious,' the new ministry that is Mary Ann's legacy. It is dedicated to providing support and help to cancer patients and their families and provide the way to peace, God and happiness through the power of prayer. Mary Ann provided instructions to her family and friends for all the details of this ministry. Today, we are sharing with others what Mary Ann shared with us; the gift of hope that comes from knowing and loving God.

STORY WRITTEN BY ROLANDO MARCHIS

Continuing the Legacy

At about 9.30 p.m. PDT (Pacific Daylight Time) on Sunday, 25 July 2010, I was in front of my computer doing some work and I received an e-mail coming from Imelda Butler, asking that I call her. In that same e-mail, she briefly informed me that there had been an accident involving John, but no more information or details were shared.

Given that the e-mail was sent to me at about 5.30 a.m. in Ireland, where Imelda was, I had an immediate sense that something bad had happened to John. I thought something like a car accident or some other accident of a serious nature had happened, but I wasn't thinking that John had passed away. When I called and spoke with Imelda, and was told that John had been stung by a wasp, and that he had a reaction to it, I was thinking the next words were going to describe his situation in the hospital and how he was doing, but when Imelda said he passed away, I was completely shocked. I wasn't prepared nor expecting that news. I just screamed, yelled, 'No! No! No! No! It can't be! It can't be! Tell me, it is not true! John can't be dead.'

I couldn't believe it. However, after speaking with Imelda further, while I still couldn't believe it, his death immediately started to set in as real. I broke down and cried.

Thus, on Sunday, 25 July 2010, my life and how I viewed it changed. My friend, colleague and mentor, John Butler, whom I had known for eight years, with whom I had a strong and significant relationship, who I had spoken with almost daily for the last year and a half, had suddenly, and tragically, passed away.

Thus, on the afternoon of Sunday, 25 July 2010, John Butler was in his garden, on his estate in Kildare, Ireland where he and his wife, life and business partner, Imelda Butler, so often enjoyed spending time together. That while in his garden, on that Sunday afternoon, John was dead-heading roses when he was stung by a wasp on his finger. He had an anaphylactic shock reaction to the sting and within about ten minutes, had passed away in his garden.

118

My journey since that day has been to continue the legacy of John Butler. John was a world-class consultant, mentor, author, advisor and the architect of *Odyssey: The Business of Consulting*. He had helped many people around the world become better by addressing their own issues, fears and problems, in professional, business and personal environments.

As we worked together, closely for the last eighteen months prior to his passing, his influence and mentoring of me was of significant impact. We had conversations, almost daily, about the business. He mentored me and many times we laughed together and even screamed at each other and I always knew that John cared about me personally, no matter what we talked about.

As the President of Odyssey Transformational Strategies, I am engaged in keeping his legacy alive, by continuing to focus on the passion that John had for helping others, by advising clients and consultants alike, to do better, be better and have a greater positive impact on their people and clients.

As I continue the legacy by managing the Odyssey business, there doesn't pass a day where I don't hear John's words regularly speaking to me about a particular client situation. John and I have spoken about so many aspects of this business in the past and, as similar issues come up today, I can hear his words of prior discussions very clearly, coming back to me today.

I often have sad moments and get teary-eyed, when I think of John not being here anymore. On some occasions, I have actually had to completely stop what I was doing, as an overwhelming level of emotion took over.

Thus, there are days when those sad moments come, sometimes after talking about John's methodologies to others and sometimes for no real apparent reason at all. It is an ongoing journey of remembrance of John and sadness for my loss of him.

As I have put thought to this actual document, I have found some struggle and some solace in writing it. In that, I don't know why such a larger-than-life man, such as John Butler, who positively impacted on so many people all over the world, was so needlessly and so suddenly taken away from us all. It is still unbelievable and his death makes no sense to me.

As I reflect upon John's influence, I realise that he is still with me, in my heart, my head and my soul, so while he has physically left us, his essence, his spirit, his wisdom and his intellect will never be gone to me.

The grieving for me is not over. I am not sure it ever will be, and I know that John will always be with me, for the rest of my life.

Due to the kind of relationship we had, I know that his words and the wisdom he shared with me will continue to be with me during many critical times in my life. Like an angel on my shoulder, he will be there and speak to me. I know this.

If there are any learnings to share with others, it is nothing earth-shattering, but simply that it is OK to cry about losing someone special. I feel it is normal and absolutely part of the grieving process and there is no need to make excuses for it. It is also OK to recognise the loss and to take the time, whatever time you need, to process it in your way.

I believe that, at some point, I will come to some understanding of why John left us and hope that by then, the grieving will also be less.

I know that his 'hand, head, heart and soul' are always with me and, for that I feel happy and privileged for having the benefit of working with and knowing my friend, colleague and mentor, John Butler.

Delights of Happy Memories

The story of this relationship begins in our local shop with the eighteen-year-old student working the summer holidays.

It progresses from there with an invitation for Siobhan to come for an evening meal after work. This is an interesting start to the relationship as she is a vegetarian, but one who loves her desserts.

And so began a friendship and some years of a very loving relationship with one young person who was very much loved by this family, to the extent that some people in the parish thought she lived with us.

Siobhan had now made friends with a family where all the siblings had left home and in a jocular fashion she considered herself to be the baby of this new household she had befriended. So many happenings, queuing all night for tickets to the U2 Croke Park concert of June 2005, Bruce Springsteen in the RDS, the theatre for the play on the troubled Saipan episode and the tears from Siobhan when we went to the cinema to view *The Wind that Shakes the Barley*. The storyline of this film made a lasting impression on her.

There was more to her life than spending all her time with us. She travelled to Australia and New Zealand, spent lots of time with her friends, played poker, enjoyed the Punchestown races, and loved to spend Sundays in Croke Park when Kildare played there.

She was a volunteer with the local Arch Club; how many boxes she filled for the shoebox appeal at Christmas will never be known.

She trained with the local Bethany Bereavement Group and once a year was involved with the Bereavement in Barretstown Gang and she spent two weeks working with the Moldavian Orphanage Group.

Sundays have now settled into a routine. By 10.20 a.m. the text arrives to say she is on her way to attend Mass at 11.00 a.m.,

121

pay a visit to the local shop and home to prepare lunch. In the afternoon, it was a delight for her to take us for a Sunday drive. We had the most super times going out, for on so many occasions we never knew where we were going.

But we did get to some very memorable places, Slieve Bloom mountains, with lunch in Kinnity Castle, the Rock of Dunamaise, several trips to Glendalough, one of which was memorable; It was a walk to the skyline and an encounter with a wild goat.

When we returned to the car park, with tears in her eyes she turned to kiss both of us as, in her words, she had achieved it with two people whom she loved very much. It was a walk she would not have done with her peers, thinking it was beyond her, as she had a weight problem.

Christmases were a wonderful time and the cause of great fun.

However, health problems loomed large on the horizon. Firstly it was the removal of an ovary, and the results were looking good. However, near the close of the year the diagnosis was one of cancer. Chemo followed, she had just started treatment when in a casual phone call she asked me to shave off her hair.

Dear God, this was the most difficult thing I had to do. I said 'Yes' quickly as I didn't want her to know the pain that act caused me. She was very matter of fact about it, didn't want clumps of hair on her pillow. When she was not in hospital, Sundays still had the same routine. She clung so fiercely to her independence, in between being hospitalised. Her Sunday lunches were now more organised, with the main course eaten and a rest period before dessert.

We continued life as normal, death was never spoken about, birthdays were celebrated. We now entered a new phase in which her death was now closer than we ever wanted to think about.

On Sunday 1 March Siobhan paid her last visit to our home. By this stage she was no longer able to drive. Her life ended on 16 March at the age of twenty-four and five months. The attendance at the removal and to the graveyard was a testament to the life she had lived.

The days of sorrow and sadness were difficult ones, and none more difficult than Sunday, because it was such a special one.

I know many people are unaccepting of the very idea that those who have gone before us are able to let us know that all is well with them in their heavenly home.

However, in May, two months after her passing at 11.55 a.m., I shall never forget the most magnificent perfume of flowers that fleetingly passed through our kitchen. From that day on we were able to accept her death. But she remains much loved and spoken about by everyone she had come to know while she had been in our home and company. Many times we visit her grave on birthdays, anniversaries, Christmas and especially summer.

And we stand and pray for this wonderful young person who was part of our life for such a short period, but who left us with a wealth of memories.

My Neighbours & Male Friends

This is the story about my male neighbours, one to the West and one to the East. Men are not always good at making friends but I was blessed with two male neighbours, both very different in character, who were to leave this world in their mid-fifties; leaving this male with time to reflect and wonder.

Looking West

Benny built his house on the adjoining site in the west in 1989 and so the relationship began. Benny was a man who seemed to enjoy life to the full and had a great network of friends. A vet by training, Benny had a wide range of interests from aeroplanes to vintage cars to music. In fact he was a walking encyclopaedia. When he took on a subject he embraced it with enthusiasm, this included music. He had an eclectic taste in music, including the Bogmen, who became infamous through their inability to hold a tune. For three years we searched for a copy of their tape until rescued through the John Creedon show on RTÉ Radio One, who put out a call on our behalf. Benny loved to have friends around him and was always generous with his time. When he built a villa in Nerja, Spain, his wish was to have friends at close quarters.

Benny at age fifty-five needed keyhole surgery, which turned into a team of almost twenty theatre staff lifting his liver to effect a repair. For twelve months Benny nursed an enormous, slow-healing scar. When on the threshold of recovery, and a new career, he died suddenly of a stroke on 4 July. I was shocked at a death so unexpected and to realise that all the plans we had for the future came to nothing in a moment.

We would plan and speculate for tomorrow. However, I did not always live the moment. Yet Benny planned the future and lived the moment by sharing his generosity of time with others. His waking after his death helped me cope, although it has left a void, for sharing ideas, speculating for the future and looking forward to increasing our interdependence as over the future years Nerja, Spain would become 'home'. I could no longer look west or feel challenged by the walking encyclopaedia and friend that was Benny.

Looking East

I had become acquainted with the Butler family through our common interest in consultancy and the Training Institution throughout the 1980s. When the house to our east became vacant and we heard the Butler family had expressed an interest some years previous, I rang a local auctioneer and said find me a good neighbour, suggesting the Butlers.

John was the eternal optimist whose first thought was his family, the 'girls' who were the apple of his eye. When it came to life in general and business in particular, he believed in the art of the possible and was always a positive thinker.

John loved his sport and many a rugby match we watched, roaring and shouting at the TV with copious helpings of hospitality. In sport he never forgot his Gaelic roots and at his all too soon funeral his roots did not forget him.

John had an inbuilt inner body clock which hit a wall of tiredness at 10.00 p.m. It was time to let the great man have his rest. This was understandable, as he frequently arose at 5.00 a.m. to write the business books he became famous for.

John loved his garden and his hot tub. He crammed a lot into his life and in his spare moments was devoted to family and his garden. You could hear John working in the garden from early on weekend mornings and he would give a roar of delight as he eased himself into the hot tub.

I have only known warm welcomes, good humour and generous hospitality in his company. He loved to share his garden with his friends and could muster a Kelly workforce to help prepare for the big outdoor barbecues.

The shock of all this life coming to a sudden and dramatic stop on a beautiful sunny day in his beloved garden from a wasp sting is difficult to comprehend.

It is the suddenness of John's death that has led to disbelief and even denial that this could come to pass. It was the two days of his waking that helped to bring reality of the loss and the associated healing that gives. There is guilt in being left behind, there is anger for the injustice of his death and incomprehension of the world order that lets such events happen.

There is new resolve to enjoy everyday as it comes, as John would.

While I love the company of the women in my life, I miss the man I called neighbour.

Soul Sisters Journey Connection

In 1994, on a recommendation from a mutual friend, MaryScott King, along with her mother MaryLisle, came for private sessions with me. MaryScott was hobbling on crutches on the start of a vacation with her mother. For years we have talked about our first session. She said: 'I have a great house, a great job, great friends, I am miserable.' 'Great', I said to her, 'So when do we get started, Sherry?' I said to this amazing woman: 'We just did!' You and I know exactly where you are.' She had no idea, just like many people, how amazing she was. Being amazed by herself would unfold as we began MaryScott's healing journey at the Quantum Pathic Center of Consciousness.

At that first meeting, I had no idea how much my life would evolve because of her. To say that during these next six years, I could not even imagine that we would become Soul Sisters at the deepest level of connection. This was, at the time, not even an idea for me when she made her appointment to see me. In those first moments, as MaryScott laid on my 'healing' bed, in her initial experience delving deep inside of her self, we connected with our souls. Neither one of us would have thought that a soul sister would show up at my door in 1994 and that both our lives would be changed forever.

Over the next six years, MaryScott attended classes at the centre regularly. She was an inspiration to all who met her here. She would delve deeply into her issues at her core. She strived to find her answers and knew without questioning that she would find them inside of her self. Like everything in life, there is always the process. Actually she would laugh about the process. One of her comments to me was: 'A process is like going into the hotdog rendering plant and coming out the other end encased in the same old stuffing.' So she said we were only going to progressively process together. She would get the lessons, figure it out and move forward. I was there to support her in her 'progressive process'.

Through these years as our friendship grew, I watched MaryScott transform her life with purpose, on purpose. She had complained many times in the beginning of not being recognised at work. She was very responsible and took her job seriously, sometimes too seriously. An achiever all the way! At one point she told me she was considering another company. I asked her: 'Is this a lateral move?' She said, 'Yes, it is.'

You must see that you are sending out the 'poor me' vibes: 'No one is recognising me.' 'You are not stating your truth and not asking for what you would like to do in this company. Stop blaming your boss or anybody else. Step up to the plate and recognise your self, not through your ego but through your deep inner self respect and knowledge from your experience.' After several conversations, MaryScott got 'it'.

She began to look at her self in a different way. She saw her self as a contributor, a viable team member with great ideas to offer her company. She stood up inside her self and validated her self from her heart. Literally from that moment, her career changed as she stood in her power. During the next several years, she was given raises, promotions and was recognised for her contribution to her company.

One of the more memorable facets of MaryScott was her wonderful ability to connect to people. She would listen intently to what they had to say. Even if she didn't agree, she would consider their viewpoint and say to her self: 'I wonder what I am learning from this experience?' Her ardent quest for understanding was miraculous to watch. She never missed a beat. The more conscious MaryScott became, the more joy you could see in her eyes, in her body language and in her manner. Judgement of her self and others became less and less until it was gone from her consciousness.

Shopping – oh yes, shopping – this was our most fun connection. MaryScott on her sojourns to Scottsdale were not just to take the classes and private sessions, they were to SHOP with capital letters.

We shopped, we ate, we laughed and we dressed MaryScott to the hilt. This was one of many adventures in which we indulged hunting for bargains. We both agreed we were born under the dollar sign with the sale sign as our rising sun. We had wondrous repeated patterns of great times, bling-collecting, accessorising and, most of all, shoes. We both shared this common bond – shoes!

During her many adventures here, MaryScott introduced her sister HelenLisle to Quantum Pathic. Another soul sister friendship was born. HelenLisle wrote the Quantum Pathic Theme song, writing the words from her heart as she connected heart to heart with her sister, and me too. Watching the two of these sisters bond with such depth beyond the biology, the genes and the family experiences, these two gals created a relationship of newness keeping the best of their pasts and letting go of the 'stuff' that was done and over. It was inspiring to watch these real sisters become in-depth soul sisters and love each other so much more deeply without any past issues or trauma dramas. They got each other without any judgement. So fabulous to be a part of their soul journey.

Carlo was the love of MaryScott's life. They dated, went through several courses of trauma dramas as many couples do, shared in each other's passion for snowboarding. Carlo is the snowboarder extraordinaire. In one of the funniest phone calls I received from MaryScott in her journey to consciousness, she was complaining about Carlo. She told me what she had said to him and wanted my opinion of what she 'should do'. After listening to the details of her conversation with Carlo, I expressed to her that she owed him an apology. 'What?' MaryScott said very loudly over the phone. 'You asked my opinion. You were out of line.' She said in a very disgruntled voice: 'I thought you were on my side?' I told her I was on her side. After she calmed down, looked at the facts after all her emotions cleared, she laughed. 'Of course I owe him an apology.' She thanked me profusely, we laughed, she hung up! Carlo received his apology and they were back on track. She lovingly took responsibility for her self.

There are so many experiences that MaryScott and I shared. She once said to me: 'Sherry, all experiences teach us.' For sure, MaryScott, wherever you are, I know in my heart you are still having amazing experiences. In January 2010, MaryScott and

Carlo were in Colorado doing their favourite sport, snowboarding, through the forest and the mountains. They were taking their sport to a new level, jumping from a helicopter right into their run. Carlo usually went first but MaryScott led the way. All along her run, she soared. There is a saying that there are no accidents. Yet as MaryScott crossed a creek, she slipped and fell. Her helmet caught in some rocks and in less than ten inches of water, MaryScott drowned. As though peacefully fulfilled with her life, for whatever reason, MaryScott transitioned.

The funeral director, a forensic scientist with twenty-five years' experience, said she had never 'worked' with a person so clear, so clean and so pure as MaryScott. One of MaryScott's favourite expressions was: 'Live, love and laugh.' In the funeral home, on the wall outside of her room, her favourite saying was on the wall. There were so many coincidences in her death just like in her life. She even connected with the funeral director, who was so impressed by this youthful, seemingly full of life woman who had a freak accident. Was it really a freak accident or planned by MaryScott's fate? In one of her last messages to me she said she was the happiest person, felt fulfilled and so grateful for everyone in her life. Perhaps this was a premonition. I can't say for sure.

After her death, MaryScott's mother gave me one of her journals that I will treasure for the rest of my life. In her journal she wrote: 'MS found her laugh with Sherry – Way Shower. I love my life, I feel in love with my self!' She made a promise to me that she would spend her fifty-first birthday at the centre as she did her fiftieth celebration. She didn't make it in body, but she was there in spirit. At her fiftieth birthday party, we celebrated like young teenagers. We had a PJ Party, celebrating part of the evening under the stars, sharing wonderful food, a special birthday cake, lots of perfect MaryScott gifts, celebrating her life as well as the lives of those who attended. A special time was had by all. MaryScott was and still is a Way Shower.

Oh yes, we did celebrate her fifty-first birthday with a celebration of MaryScott's life. Everyone who attended shared a personal experience about her. We all laughed, cried and remembered her. For sure, I miss our adventures together. There is no one I know at this moment who loves to shop as much as I do. But it is not quite the same anymore. I miss my friend very much. I miss the laugh she found with me. I miss her laughter and her great sense of humour. But I know she lives in my heart with the memories of the great soul sister experiences we shared. I will never forget you, MaryScott. At times, I feel her presence and her message comes through loud and clear: 'Live, laugh and love.' I love you MaryScott and thank you for coming into my life. You brightened many of my days. In gratitude, gratefulness and thankfulness to you for coming into my life. I love and miss you, dear soul sister. I know I will see you again.

Courage to Step Across the Rubicon Bridge

I was given the topic 'Change Management' to facilitate as part of the Rubicon Workshop. I chose to take the group through an experiential activity around 'Change' as I was more comfortable with experiential learning than I was with classroom teaching. I asked everyone to get out of their chairs and come to the back of the room. I noticed a sceptical glare from John.

The group paired up and the instructions were to turn away from your partner and change five pieces of your clothing. When you turned around your partner would look up and down and state what he/she had changed in their appearance. John in his way gave a couple of comments that weren't very welcoming to this new way of learning. Once each partner had completed their observations I asked them to change seven new items. Well, John had already changed back to his original self. He moaned and groaned and gave it another go. 'I don't have enough clothes to make any more changes', he responded. Again after the pairs had made their observations for the second time I asked them to change ten more items for the third and final round of change. Again John had already changed back to his tidy self and was ready to move on. He was quite vocal about all the changes he had to make to satisfy the requirement of ten changes. I ended the exercise and gathered the group into a circle to debrief the activity.

The point of this activity is to have people recognise that when there is nothing left to change creativity emerges. People were giving each other their shoes, belts, jewellery, jackets, sweaters and having lots of fun in the process.

My question to the group: What did you notice about yourself as more and more change was asked of you? How does this reflect how you deal with change in your work/home environment?

I asked John directly in front of the group: 'John do you have trouble making change in your work/home environment?'

He quickly responded that he was very open to the change process. I asked again if this was the truth … He then turned to Imelda and asked: 'Do I have trouble with change?' Imelda had a big smile and in her loving way just kept smiling. I think he finally got it. We all had a good laugh.

I don't know if he really got it but for the first time in my relationship with John I felt as though I could teach people of his caliber something new.

John gave me the *courage* to step across the Rubicon Bridge.

I miss him …

CHAPTER FIVE

Children's Stories

A thousand words won't bring you back I know because I've tried,
neither will a million tears I know because I've cried.

Most people expect that our mother and father should live forever. However, the harsh reality is that life is very short even if our parents do live to be a hundred years old. They are still our parents and we seldom envisage a life without their knowing presence and understanding love.

Along with time, comes an acceptance and understanding that we will grieve for our parents for the rest of our lives, each in our own way. As a tribute to their love and guidance we espouse the respect and values they displayed in their lives.

Let us mark the special occasions in our lives and in our children's lives with the wonderful memories of love which we cherish from our parents, so we live the legacy, learn the lessons and become all that we were born to be. Let us live each day with zest as Hubert recommends in his story. Let those who love you help you along the journey.

The following stories of life and love and death and suffering and grieving are spoken from the heart of each contributor. We hope you receive peace, hope and consolation in the passages of stories told by children whose parents have died.

Your Eternal Smile

Dear Dad,

I find it hard to express our connection – it was perfect. I love you so deeply, so purely and so unconditionally. I looked up to you and I am inspired by you. I felt like your little Ria all the time. I understood you totally because we were so alike. Time with you was the best! You were my teacher in life and in your sudden, untimely and tragic death, you continued to teach me so much.

Yours always, Ria

I never knew or understood, actually I never even imagined, before 25 July 2010, the depth of the pain that engulfs you when you lose a loved one so unexpectedly. For me, 25 July 2010 was the day that life changed when I lost my beloved Dad. I was heartbroken, truly. I felt broken and since that day I have been working on mending the broken-heartedness.

Looking back now over the last months and my experience, I believe part of the brokenness is helped in the hours, days and weeks following sudden death. Although the pain is raw and overpowering, rather surreal and yet real at the same time, and the feelings are intense and uncontrollable, there are special moments of beauty in those initial hours, days and weeks.

For me, one of those moments came when I saw him for the first time, my adored Dad, lying there: still, cold, but with a distinct smile on his face, and I was overpowered by a deep sense of serenity. Dad was certainly present in that bare mortuary and he was peaceful. I knew that. Seeing him, and particularly with a smile, truly was a beautiful emotion because it was so him. It brought a sense of fullness when I looked at him. It was perfect in a way that is beyond words.

There were a few of those moments of pure serenity and peace and beauty in those initial days of pain. They were moments of grief but of light in the darkness. Those moments of strength helped me to survive, to keep breathing and in ways to grow. In the days following Dad's death they gave me strength to survive the floods of tears and words; the uncertainty and the absolution; the hustle of the event, the noise and the deafening silence; the chronic fatigue, dizziness and the haunting headaches; the emptiness of forgetting and the weight of remembering his death; and all the memories of yesterday and realisation that tomorrow is forever changed.

Be not afraid, because your loved one has completed their purpose. I believe in that and it helped me. I felt in a way it was my Dad's perfect passing and I looked for signs to reaffirm that. I found his handwritten 'purpose' on a small post-it note in his wallet and it was true – eerily so! He had completed what he had written on the small note. It made sense to me in that moment. Again he was my teacher. His purpose read (in part): 'My purpose is to become one with my wild nature (ironically, he died in his garden after a fatal reaction to a wasp sting!); to find my true path in life and to help others find their path (I believe that he was content. He guided Mam, Shell and I to where we are!) When I read it I knew that he had completed it and I was happy for me and proud of him but sad he was gone. I think we all have to find ways to struggle through those hours and days and help ourselves understand the pain and passing and the trauma. Sometimes little things appear and for me it helped to believe in my Dad and his own words.

The funeral was almost like an out of body experience and all the emotions were overpowering. The strangest thing in those hours was not Dad at all, but the other people (my Mam, my sister, extended family, friends, neighbours) and their pain, their tears and reactions. Dealing with the reactions of your dearest loved ones is so difficult during those moments, hours and days following a sudden death. Some moments, you are in total denial and your family member is hysterical and you don't know what to do because in that moment you don't feel anything. It happened to me a few times. I can still hear the crying of my sister, Michelle, I can still feel her pain and my instinct was to help her and heal her but it is so hard to do.

I learned that how you connect with your closest loved ones in those moments, hours and days is important. I remember Mam saying that we need to forgive each other for things we say and do in those hours and not take everything personally. She was very right! Also remembering that everyone deals with the shock and grief differently. I learned in the months following that grief is so unique, that it's hard to ever really understand another's pain but it is critical to understand that we are all different and healing is different. That is something that is so obvious in life but when facing death it is hard to remember.

For me, Dad's youngest daughter, who had just turned twenty-six years old when I got 'The Call'. I was over 3000 miles away from the epicentre when he died in our cherished garden with his soulmate, my Mam. I was 3000 miles away when he was rushed to our local hospital and when my sister and extended family arrived on the scene. I have been living in the US for a few years and I was not expecting 'That Call' about my healthy and energetic fifty-five year old father. Some sort of angels got me the 3000 miles home to Ireland that Sunday (a three hour drive from Albany, NY where I was speaking at a conference, twenty minutes to pack and get to the airport and a seven hour flight to Dublin). Agonisingly, the angels could not prevent the physical pain and torture that was so devastating every single mile home. I don't know if I could ever advise people about the pain because it is excruciating but somehow you have to allow yourself be.

When I got home early on the Monday morning (26 July), we went straight to the hospital and I saw my Dad and his special smile, and then we took him home to our family home. It was all so confusing for me because only seven short weeks earlier, we had celebrated our beautiful magical family wedding (5 June 2010) at home – the same garden where Dad had died. All the memories, the scenes, the people, the intensity were similar in ways but we were now at the very bottom. It was almost too much to comprehend or understand or survive. My adored Dad walked me down the aisle with his teary eyes – and the next time I walked into that same local familiar church, the church of my childhood and my special wedding day – I was walking him, my amazing Dad, down that same aisle, in a box we had chosen yesterday. It was awful! The combination, the extremes, the juxtaposition was too much to comprehend.

Most days I still can't make sense of it and the brokenness is held together by band-aids. Perhaps time will help at some point, people seem to think that or at least, people seem to say that. Right now, I get offended and saddened by time passing because it seems to me that moving further away makes it more permanent and less present. I am beginning to understand that loss and grief and compassion do not stop as time moves away, but they change. I have learnt that losing someone you love is a deep understanding of others and we must all remember to reach out, acknowledge and support others regardless of how long ago the death occurred.

I know my Dad was a believer in life and I still hear his simple phrase: 'Trust the process, Ria.' Grief, death and mending the broken-heartedness are part of life's process and at points you have to just 'trust in that process', and keep breathing and living, and keep learning, even from the hardest moments.

LIFE – *Living In Fearless Existence*

C.S. Lewis said 'Experience is a brutal teacher, but you learn. My God, do you learn'.

My dad John died on 25 July 2010 at the age of 55 years old. I was half his age at 27 years old and most certainly did not feel equipped to deal with this sudden and unexpected loss.

Writing this, I struggled to find words to express the unspeakable, thoughts of the unthinkable, the absolute unimaginable and feelings too colossal to narrow down in words.

I learnt that when devastation stung my life, that my soul needed creative means to expel grief. This is a tribute I've written about my dad.

<u>My Dad</u>

You are twice my age and a million times my inspiration
And lived by your motto 'Live well, Laugh often, Leave a Legacy'

You are the champion cheerleader to my good deeds
And the watchful eye over my misdeeds.

You are the protector of our Clan and our 'little piece of heaven'
And my secure base.

You are the anam cara (soul friend) to my mum
And a crucial cornerstone to our family of four.

You are the BBQ host at the heart of our extended family
And the charismatic joker in a flowery shirt.

You are my accomplice for a sneaky pint
And last minute delegator of your Christmas shopping!!

You are my shadow side and inner voice
And the judge of my culinary experiments.

You are worldwide, a guru and visionary to millions
And at home, the ruler of the remote control!!

You are the early starter to every dawn
And the suspected finisher of the Ferrero Rocher!!

You are the Chief of 'The Apostrophe Association'
And the chief brainstormer of all my projects.

You are at one with your wild nature.
You are my hero. My dad.

Dad, I miss you. I love you.
You are gone but you are always in my heart.

At the funeral, I read a passage from his book, *Crossing the Rubicon – Seven Steps to Writing Your Own Personal Strategy*.
The sentiment seemed to say perfectly the advice my dad would give to me and everyone at a difficult time.

Promise Yourself:

To be so strong that nothing can disturb your peace of mind

To talk health, happiness and prosperity to every person you meet

To tell all your friends that there's something in them

To look at the sunny side of everything and make your optimism come true

To think only the best, to work only for the best and to expect only the best

To be just as enthusiastic about the success of others as you are about your own

To forget the mistakes of the past and press on to greater achievements of the future

To wear a cheerful face at all times and give every creature you meet a smile

To give so much time to the improvement of yourself that you have no time to criticize others

To be too large for worry, too noble for anger, too strong for fear and too happy to permit the presence of trouble

To think well of yourself and proclaim this fact to the world not in loud words but in great deeds.

To live in the faith that the whole world is on your side so long as you are true to the best that is in you.

My dad's life advice was 'trust the process'.

When he died I was half his age. I learnt that, if it's half time already, I better get busy living LIFE in fearless existence.

STORY WRITTEN BY RUSSELL J. WATSON, ED.D.

Daddy, can I touch the moon tonight?

A lunar perigee happens about once every twenty years. We non-astronomers call it a 'supermoon'. It's when the moon is nearly ten per cent closer to earth, and it appears almost fifteen per cent bigger in the sky. The moon always looks larger at the horizon, and when a supermoon occurs, it's huge and it makes news. One of those happened in early December when I was five years old.

As the supermoon began to rise above the hillside at the back of our house in New Athens, Ohio, it seemed to fill the sky as I looked across the snow covered field. 'Daddy, can I touch the moon tonight?', I called with excitement. I wasn't certain that I could, but it looked so close that maybe if Daddy held me on his shoulders, I could try to be the first. (Okay, psychologists reading this, please know that I was an early five-year-old, and that's pre-conservation age for boys, according to Erik Erikson. For non-psychologists, it just means that young kids are clueless about some things, distance being one of them. Clueless, not stupid, their brains can't dig certain concepts at young ages.) I was beginning to reason this, even as I asked the question, but I recall imagining being held on Daddy's shoulders and maybe almost touching the moon. Dad could have said something like: 'No, it's impossible.' Instead, he said: 'Sure, let's try to do it!'

Moonrise doesn't last very long. I recall being quickly bundled into snowsuit, boots, gloves, hood, scarf, a process that a five-year-old is not very adept at doing, so both Mom and Dad worked the process to a snug completion. Dad got my sled; I jumped on in waist-deep snow for me, and knee-deep snow for him. The supermoon still loomed very large at the top of the hill, which was about 400 yards away. The trip up the hillside was a slow one, Dad was pulling my sled as fast as he could, but Dad wasn't feeling well, but I didn't realise that at the time.

A teachable moment

As we finally reached the crest of the hill, the moon was fully off the horizon, yet still very large in the sky. I was disappointed, but

Dad put me on his shoulders and I reached into the air, realising that my wish for touching the supermoon was virtually impossible. He explained to me that the moon was very far away, and that when the moon is on the horizon, it looks like it's very close to the earth, but it's still very far away. Dad had a teachable moment with me, and he seized it. He patiently helped me through my pre-conservation, Eriksonian reasoning by showing me how to think through the process. It was a vivid teachable moment from a patient father.

Christmas, and a field trip for Dad
A few weeks later, Christmas arrived and it was a memorable one. Even though we didn't have much money, I found my first electric train under the Christmas tree. It was a very special gift from Santa, and one that was certainly planned and budgeted for earlier in the year. A few weeks later, in mid-January, the Christmas tree was gone, and the train remained in full and careful use. I was playing with the train and Dad came over to me, knelt down to give me a hug and a kiss, and said: 'Daddy loves you very much and I'm going to the hospital for a while.' I said: 'Okay, Daddy, I love you too.' I didn't know much about what had just been said, or what it meant. I remember waving to Dad as he was driven down the driveway.

Dad wasn't feeling well because he had a difficult illness that was puzzling to diagnose. The young soldiers in World War II called dad one of the 'old men'. He enlisted into the US Navy at age thirty-three as World War II began. He was a good swimmer, and could have stayed at the Navy base in San Diego, California and taught swimming to the teenagers who were enlisting. Then, those who were fighting the war in combat would have called him a 'slacker'. He was never a slacker, and didn't want to be called one. Dad was assigned to a medical unit in Guadalcanal and was in charge of refrigeration of medicines and blood. Dad spent the war maintaining medical refrigeration units, and that meant spending most days covered in oil and Freon, as well as other chemical refrigerants used in the 1940s, which have now (decades later) been linked to cardiac and nervous system complications. It was probably some of the long-term effects from these chemicals that were breaking down Dad's health and well-being. As a five-year-old boy, I was clueless, and largely remained clueless, as children weren't allowed into hospitals to visit during the 1950s. It simply wasn't done. I really wish I could have seen him in the hospital, with the tubes, machines, and medical staff. It would have helped me understand the gravity of the situation.

My Valentine for Dad

Valentine's Day was near, and Mom was at the hospital. Aunt Evelyn, who was staying with me at our house helped me make a Valentine for Dad. I dictated a brief note for Aunt Evelyn to write: 'Daddy, I love you. When you get home from the hospital, let's build a snow fort together in the back yard. Happy Valentine's Day.' I know exactly what the Valentine said, because I have it now. It was one of the things that Dad saved while at the hospital.

Less than a month later, on 1 March, the snow had melted, and I was with my cousin Tom flying a kite in the early spring winds. I was with Tom and his Mom, Aunt Lottie, for the day as Mom had to go to the hospital very quickly. Mom returned to the yard that afternoon in tears, and said: 'Russy, God had to take your Daddy home to be with him.' At the time, I wasn't certain what that meant. As a five-year old, I didn't know much about what was going on and what was happening. I knew that people were upset, but I didn't fully comprehend what was really happening at the time.

At the funeral

I recall going to Dad's funeral and seeing him in the casket. I still didn't realise or understand what had taken place. The funeral directors had prepared Dad's body for an open casket viewing. I remember that it seemed like they had him painted and made up like a matinee idol in the theatre. I'd never seem my Dad in make-up, powder and lipstick; it seemed unusual and even perhaps silly to me. I remember others at the funeral, Aunt Lottie, especially, crying profusely, almost to the point of not knowing if she was laughing or crying. She was crying very heavily, as she was my Dad's older sister and they were very close. I was still puzzled, and Mom was in the midst of her own sudden grief, and tried to comfort me by saying that Daddy was now going to be with God. I was taught that God was good, so that must be an okay thing. Someone had coached Mom not to take me to the burial service at the cemetery, a decision that later on she said she regretted. Perhaps going to the burial service, I would have finally understood. As we prepared to leave the funeral home that evening, Mom took me by the hand to Dad's casket, and said: 'Say goodbye to your Daddy.' I remember asking: 'Mommy, will he hear me?' Mom said: 'Yes, he'll hear you,' and she cried. I don't remember if I said goodbye to Dad, as much as I've thought about it, I can't recall.

Dad took the time ...

Dad took the time to be with me when I was a very small boy. He took me to the park, to the swings; we had footraces to let the winner choose if we had pancakes or waffles for breakfast. He even took me up the long hill in the winter so that I could try to touch the moon, even when he wasn't feeling well, and knowing that what I asked to do was impossible. All of these moments could have been put off until later, at which point, I would have no memories of my Dad. I hope that I have learned from my Dad's example, and I hope that I've taken the appropriate time to spend with my children, Justin and Lindsey, as they've grown; they are now young adults. Only they can answer that question.

Finally, touching the moon

In 1984, I was about ten years into my career as a psychology teacher. President Ronald Reagan announced in his State of the Union speech that a teacher would be selected to go on a Space Shuttle mission in January, 1986. I applied immediately. So did 100,000 other teachers. Only 10,000 completed the long writing involved in the application process and I was one of the 10,000 who took the time, thought, and effort to complete it. I was fortunate enough to be selected through additional cuts, and I made it to the top 100 of the semi-finalists out of the 10,000 applicants. We were flown to the Kennedy Space Center in October of 1985 to watch the launch of the shuttle scheduled prior to the 'Teacher in Space' Challenger mission in January, 1986. Krista McAuliffe, the teacher who died with the other astronauts in the Challenger explosion was in the audience with us as we watched the successful launch. During the week we were at the Space Center as semi-finalists, many of our teachers and presenters were the astronauts who flew there. Additionally, we were certified by NASA to handle and demonstrate lunar material samples (moon rocks) for schools and colleges. I couldn't believe that slightly over thirty years after I asked my Dad if he could help me touch the moon from that hilltop in Ohio, that I would actually hold lunar samples in my hands. I thought of Dad, and Mom who had passed away just seven years prior to the NASA experience. I felt very blessed for the hilltop field trip with my Dad, and blessed to have the honour to hold priceless pieces of the moon in my hands. (The lunar samples are encased in plastic, and all carefully numbered and recorded, but nonetheless, they were in my hands then, and several times after that when I presented the moon-rocks to schools, colleges, and scout groups.) With the priceless moon rocks in my hands, I said a silent prayer of thanksgiving for the blessings I had received. Full circle in the experience, full circle of memories, and blessings with each experience.

The only question unanswered is the one that I've asked myself: 'Did I say goodbye to Dad, when Mom asked me to?' If I didn't do that then, I want to do that now. 'Goodbye, Dad. I know that you're not afraid, neither am I, and that you're in a good place. I'll see you soon. Thanks, Dad, for taking the time to spend with me when I was very young.'

Our Dad – True Family Man

Introduction

This contribution is written about our lovely late dad and we sit down to compile these words at the first anniversary of his death. As a family we are eternally grateful to Imelda and her family for this opportunity to try to put into words our experience over the last eighteen months and also for providing the opportunity to realise something positive from all the pain and sadness we have experienced. We will be happy if our account helps and resonates with even one person.

Our Dad

First and foremost dad was a true family man. His priorities always lay within the home.

Dad was a perfectionist which was sometimes a challenge for us to live up to but ultimately a worthwhile challenge that has benefited us in all aspects of our lives so far. This perfection was evident in dad's work, his garden, his beliefs and in his approach to everything he undertook.

He also took pleasure in the simple things in life. This is not something we always understood but as we mature we realise the wisdom in his approach. Dad's garden was his happy place. He could spend hours upon hours between his garage and his garden and here we saw him take pleasure in the simple things.

Dad's bravery and strength must be mentioned here. It knew no bounds and helped him fight his long battle with illness and recover from numerous knocks and setbacks while also continuing to be the person we all needed him to be. Very often we saw how much of a struggle this was for him.

Background to Dad's illness

In November 1995 dad was diagnosed with chronic renal failure on his forty-seventh birthday. No one could have predicted the roller-coaster of events and emotions that were to occur over the next fifteen years.

In March 1996 dad began treatment called haemodialysis. Haemodialysis kept dad alive. Soon after this treatment began dad was put on the transplant list. After only six weeks a suitable donor became available and dad recovered well from this life-saving surgery. In 2000 this kidney transplant failed. What followed was seven years of dialysis, failed donor matches, weeks upon weeks spent in hospitals, and endless procedures. We were watching a man who was losing hope.

On Saturday 25 August 2007 a donor kidney was found for dad. The transplant was successful and some hope was restored again in our lives.

In July 2010 dad began to complain of soreness/discomfort in his chest area. Following continued discomfort dad was sent for a scan on 17 September 2010. By 3.30 p.m., that evening the family GP was at our house carrying out what he has called one of the hardest house calls he has had to make. Our sister was at home with dad to hear heart-breaking news that it was cancer. The last thing any of us expected was cancer. There was always a sense that dad had his lot in life with kidney failure and failed transplants and we had a naïve sense that he could not be so unfortunate to suffer from another devastating disease. However, as we know life does not work out like this.

Dad's death
Dad passed away on 22 February 2010. In dad's last hour he was surrounded by his family. At different points during this last hour it seemed to us that dad struggled quite a lot. It was remarkable to watch that as the priest prayed with dad it seemed to calm him instantly and more effectively than any medication that was administered at this time. The people who were present for the hour leading up to dad's death all got the sense that something special was taking place amongst us but we cannot put words on the experience.

Dad took many breaths towards the end that we thought were his last. We recall the hospice nurse commenting that it was like dad was waiting for someone. It wasn't until his deceased brother's wife arrived and prayed with us that dad took his final breath. It is incredible that dad waited for her arrival and that on her two-hour journey she prayed to her husband for dad to wait for her. Our aunt was not aware that dad was that close to death that morning nor were we aware that she was on her way to be with dad. This whole experience has shaped our beliefs on death and dying and has positively influenced our faith.

Our grieving process

Reflecting back, a year on, we all agree that we began our grieving process the day dad got his diagnosis in September 2009. On some level, we all knew this was not going to end well. We never spoke of this instinctive fear until we had to plan bringing him home for the last time. On 22 February 2010 when dad did pass away, our initial feeling was one of relief for him and an acceptance of his death. The relief we felt was relief that dad was no longer suffering and his pain had ended. This was clear within minutes of dad passing away as he looked like his old self and not the person we had looked after for the past few months. However, in the coming weeks and months this feeling of acceptance waned and was not as prevalent for us.

Our lives and routines had revolved around the care and comfort of our dad and subsequently, in the weeks immediately after the funeral, we found ourselves idle. Our days then centred around trips to the graveyard and spending time with him there. This was a huge part of our grieving process and important in helping us through the first few days and weeks when we did not know what else to do.

It was important as time went by to take time out from the busyness of everyday life to let the reality of the loss be experienced and felt. However, this took, and still demands, a huge amount of strength and energy but it is beneficial in the long-run and, for some of us, integral to the grieving process.

In the first year we all experienced days that could probably be only described as dark days. For some of us these were characterised by feeling cheated and angry, wanting more definite explanations for what had happened, loneliness, a fear about the future, and a heavy debilitating sadness. Very often in these days there is nothing anyone can say or do to make these days better and, reflecting back on these days, perhaps this is because we did not want them to be any better and because we had to go through these dark days ourselves. These days were all part of coming to terms with the loss and the effect of the loss of our dad on our daily lives and our lives going into the future without him.

The hour leading up to dad's death was a very special and comforting experience. What we experienced the day of his death left us in no doubt that he was leaving the ones he loved here to be reunited with those who loved and had left him so many years previous. This was a huge comfort in the aftermath of his death and continues to be.

Feelings of guilt and thoughts about continuing life without Dad were very prominent in the early months and again at the first anniversary where it was hard to believe that a whole year had gone by without him.

It became apparent very early on in the grieving process that the happy events/incidents in our lives will never be as happy as they would have been if dad was around and that sad events/incidents will always be that bit more sad. There was some relief in realising and accepting this. We also realised that we wouldn't have it any other way.

The days, weeks, months after dad's death left us with so many questions that we had never seriously considered before. These questions caused great pain and anxiety and this led to a frantic search for answers. Discussions and reading books about the dying, death, people's near death experiences, the explanations for these experiences and the lack of explanations in some cases, were all very intriguing. The debates around the existence of an afterlife provided comfort in the early days and continue to do so now. It became important to determine what it is we each believed in to continue with the grieving process and to put it into some context/belief system. As we had never considered this seriously before it was an interesting journey. This journey was inspired by what we experienced in the hour leading up to dad's death.

After the first anniversary of our dad's passing there was an acceptance and understanding that we will all grieve the loss of our dad for the rest of our lives. It is difficult to explain but this brought some more comfort. We have also come to accept our pain and sadness and know that for now we would not want to be without this pain.

Lessons learnt and insights gained

There is a lot to be learned from those who are dying and from death, as well as from the complex emotions involved in grief. It is important to take the time to reflect on what lessons can be learned from such a journey. Dad devoted himself to instilling in us important values and he also taught us important life lessons. It is no surprise then that in his death he has taught us some more of these lessons.

The following points are what we have learned in the first year and want to pass on to others:

- Trust and believe in the grieving process. The grieving process is unique to every person. Trust that your body and mind will do the job of grieving at a pace it can cope with and in a way that will heal both.
- Allow yourself to cry; we found this can be a therapeutic experience that gives us the strength to continue with the grieving process.
- Talking to others who are further along the grieving process helps to feel that what you are going through is normal. It sometimes provides snapshots of what may be ahead and can be comforting.
- We have found that we prepare ourselves for the big events that happen in our lives without our dad and that this preparation is essential in helping us through these events. However, it is the small things that disarm us and cause us to experience an unexpected wave of sadness. This unexpected wave of sadness can be very debilitating.
- Books for some are an important part of the grieving process. In the early stages, books were very effective in putting words on feelings that were hard to understand, let alone express. In particular Elizabeth Kübler Ross' comforting words and experiences provided much needed

reassurance and support around the grieving process and death in general.

- There is an opportunity for growth as a result of losing a loved one. This takes time, support and reflection to achieve. For example, our experience of loss and grieving has since helped us to support and empathise with friends who have lost ones dear to them and has helped us in our professional lives. Strive to channel the sadness and loss into something positive.
- Never underestimate the importance of support from different areas in your life and trust that you get what you need when you need it.
- As time went by, we learned that life goes on but everything that is important to us remains close to us – in our hearts. We have heard time and time again that when you live in the hearts of those you love you never die. This now has meaning for us.

As a result of our experience we feel it is important to include some points for those who are close to people who are bereaved and lessons we learned about what helped us:

- Do not be afraid to talk about the deceased person with the person who is bereaved.
- If the person who is bereaved cries as a result of your conversation with them this is not a negative thing.
- Never fully believe anyone who says they are 'fine' – they're probably not.
- Remember that it does not necessarily hurt any less after a certain amount of time has passed. The support that is needed is not necessarily any less.
- Some of the most comforting conversations with friends have been the ones where they do not try to offer answers or say something to make us feel better but instead listen and ask questions that help them understand our experience of grief and the huge loss we are experiencing. Very often these questions also help the bereaved person to understand more fully their own experience also.

Final Word

The closing words from Dad's retirement speech in January 2009 were: 'No one knows what the future holds, only God knows what the future holds for anyone', and he also vowed that he was going to make the best of his retirement. Knowing what we know now about what was dad's future at the time he spoke these words, there is a valuable lesson for everyone in his words.

A heartfelt thanks to our mam, who made this difficult journey with us, for her remarkable strength and dedicated support to both dad and to us.

It's Nice to Be Nice – The Dignity, Love & Laughter of My Mam

I wonder if God cringes when he hears us use clichés. They seem to be everywhere and, try as we might, no matter the context, we all fall into the habit of using them.

My Mam died in April 2009 and I can only assume it's usual for some or all of one's senses to be heightened at and after that time. Things people said registered in their smallest detail, and I became acutely aware that sometimes we all need clichés, if only as coping mechanisms. When someone said: 'Ah, but she was a great age ... ' my eyes and heart saw the woman they'd seen as a young boy – always there, always even and fair and possibly the most nonjudgmental person I've ever known, so I'd answer, 'Yes', just to be civil. My sisters who are, like Mam before them, remarkable people, gave a great part of their time and energies to her care as the years of that 'great age' advanced – they are blessed with very special husbands and families who welcomed her into their homes during those final years. One of the girls had a lovely phrase to describe how Mam was managing towards the end: 'She's just worn out, just bunched.' I'd heard it said a few times and maybe I didn't want to notice, but when I finally saw it for myself, my heart broke and I envied God so much, thinking: 'You must really need help up there.'

'There's never a good time', or a fitting way, to prepare for that time, and no matter how much your logical self allows you to accept it, it's still – inevitably – a really difficult time. For me, other events faded into the background. I can recall being in work, going through the motions, and getting the call to tell me it would be a good time to be there – I can't remember the drive, but I vividly remember, on the way, pleading with God: 'Please don't take her until I get there', and mercifully that didn't happen.

Mam was a piano and violin teacher, but of us four siblings I

155

was the only one who didn't 'do' music properly – I'm sure she must have scratched her head and wondered what it would take to get through to me, but she was fair to me – and let me find my own way.

In 1982, ten days before my nineteenth birthday, my Dad died – to this day I have no idea how Mam coped through all the years after that, but I know her faith meant a great deal to her. What I really admire is that she never wore that as a badge, it was really much too important to allow anything like that to interfere. As in so many things, she led by her own quiet example, 'take it or leave it', find your own way, and be content that you haven't just followed the crowd.

When I think now of the period before her passing, a word keeps coming into my mind – 'dignity'. It is so necessary that it is afforded to all, but none are more deserving than those who are at that closing stage of their journey. I am forever privileged to have witnessed the love and care and dignity that my sisters gave to our Mam long before, but especially in those last days, it was an honour to have been in that presence – that of genuine humanity.

On the day Mam died I, perhaps stupidly, was consumed with worry that she'd be OK, that she'd know we were OK and that she knew we were all there with her and, most of all, that we loved her. My mind flicked back and forth between 'home', our shared past, and 'now' – I will treasure forever the memory of how she'd laugh so much that she'd shudder, and yet now, since that day, any laughs are missing a small corner, completeness is gone ... for now. So 'we soldier on' and go on living. Everyday still, for sure, I talk to Mam and I still want to know that she's OK, that she was OK and that she knows we're OK and we're thinking of and remembering her. At unexpected times I find myself staring into space and saying or asking, I really don't know which it is: 'Where are you now, Mam?'

While life does go on, it's not the same, it can't be, and there are times when the absence is consuming, but I know what Mam would say: 'Trust in the man above and just keep going.' If we're lucky we are marked by those people. We can and should carry their good into our own lives, 'take it or leave it', but no flag waving.

Mam used to tell me a story from her own youth: a simple, countryman had a rule for life that he'd tell, to anyone who would listen, with a broad smile on his face – just as she'd have when telling it to me: 'It's nice to be nice.'

Death Too Is Natural

'And now with Jesus on your right and Mary on your left, walk with them now to meet your God, who is saying: You are my son, my beloved in whom I am most proud. Daddy, you've done all God has wanted you to do on earth, you've served your purpose well, go now and take your place in heaven.'

These words I spoke to an honourable, dignified most loving gentleman whom I used to call Daddy. With my cheek resting on his, my left hand on his head, my right hand gently protecting the right hand of my father, we lay there in stillness as his soul gently passed through the cloud's veil of this world.

This was the moment I had feared the most in my life – my father dying. It had begun to be a reality from June 2008. As the nurses laid him out, my heart was filled with such love and joy as I spoke of the gift his life was to mine. How blessed I had been to have received such love from such a man. As I sat on the bed with him, holding his still-warm hands, the smile on my face was huge and just shone down in beams on him. That he had given me the last greatest gift of that precious moment of his parting will sustain me forever.

As he closed his eyes, my first thought was that death too is natural. It is a part of life. When my Dad received the Last Rites, in what was a very moving ceremony, at the end the priest asked if my Dad wished to share any last thoughts with his family. Succinctly put he said: 'It's life. I am ready to meet my God.' As there is a time for birth, so too is there a time to die. That, as my wise father summed up most concisely, is life.

I read a saying once: 'May your life be lived so that when you are born, may you cry and the world rejoice. When you die, that you rejoice and the world cry.' It was comforting to us as Dad became critical that so many shed a tear with us, consoling us in our pain of his departure that it too would be a loss to their lives. I have since reflected on that phrase since my father has passed away in a different light. Do we cry as babies when we're born as we're so sad to leave heaven and rejoice when we die as we know we are returning to our eternal home, where peace, love and joy reign eternally.

I always believed in heaven, God and Jesus but on my Dad's deathbed, the emotion that consumed me the most was, now I know there is a God. In my darkest hour, as I had feared for many years it would be, that room was filled with love, joy and immeasurable peace like nothing I had ever experienced before. There was a complete lack of sadness in my heart as my Dad passed over. That was possibly one of the biggest shocks to me, when I had expected sorrow the most, I felt it the least, all that I could feel was love.

My father had many simple philosophies on life. His one on death was simply, 'when it's your time, it's your time'. When God calls you, you must respond.

My father was seventy-seven when he passed over but he prided himself on his youthfulness and vitality for life. Many thought him fifty-five. At times in hospital the nurses called to verify his date of birth, something he revelled in sharing with us. His age was socially a state-guarded secret to the point of he insisting my mother inscribe his name only on his coffin. Sadly God must not have wanted it that way as at his removal one priest announced his date of birth to a rather wide audience, much to my father's heavenly chagrin I'm sure. Most who didn't know were shocked. My father was well known locally as the guy who walked with the umbrella. One man remarked: 'But he walked every day, he was so healthy, how did he die? That's it, I'm giving up walking!'

Maybe he followed his faith, knowing God saw what he did and that was enough for him. Knowing him though, he probably didn't even think that far, there was a job to be done, he just did it. St David, on his deathbed, encouraged others to live his life as he did, by just doing the simple things. For me, I wish to live my life by my Dad's inspiration.

My father was never an overly emotionally indulgent man. All just was as it was. He didn't waste time analysing, questioning scenarios, he just accepted whatever came his way on the day. I used to be quite the opposite, indulging sorrow, losses, pain, constantly asking: 'Why?' At times, I used to criticise my father for what I perceived to be his lack of emotion. Now I see and feel the wealth of what was his near instantaneous acceptance of what was, an ability just to accept whatever God had sent him in the day. Part of his 'dying lectures' or advice to me, was to live my life day by day, to stop worrying about the future, that I was always planning and organising, to stop all that. The future, he'd say, will take care of itself. Accept all God sends you on the day. Day by day is how you live your life.

Since he has passed over I have practised that philosophy and found it a very calm way to live. On the days when I think of a future without him in it, and the massive emotion that brings, I hear the voice: 'Now what did I tell you about worrying about the future? Focus on today only.'

It makes me wonder did my father have to die so I could learn how to live, and to live it in the fullness that he did.

I lost a significant other over a decade ago. While he's still alive, he 'died' from my living world. I lamented that loss daily for ten years but from that journey I have learnt that when you lose someone you love, you never reach a happiness that they're gone. As a newborn baby clings to their mother for love, so too are we as a race instilled with those same values and I've yet to meet anyone who will say, 'Yes I loved and was happy to have lost that love.' So it's a huge relief for me to know that I will never be happy that my father has died and will never have to take a similar journey again. My answer has arrived already. The sadness I feel at times is very acute. It stretches from my very core to the extremities of my body. In those times, even my fingers and toes feel the weight of my sadness. Other times, it's just that dull aching sadness that lingers within, that just is.

My father was always someone who comforted me physically, very demonstrative in his hugs and kisses. (I will also add that my father loved all women and was very demonstrative to all, irrespective of age, creed or dimension, in his hugs and kisses!) While I sit with that sadness, I feel a soft comfort within me that he's holding me, reassuring me that everything's going to be OK.

And that's my Dad, the alpha-male, the protector of our family still hard at work protecting his crew. We were all adored by him and always will be.

My father was so courageous in his acceptance of his death. I would not say he was happy about it but he accepted it was his time. In ways as we watched him die, I wondered was this part of it too, that he was showing us how to die, in courage, acceptance surrounded by great love. As the song says: 'Be not afraid, I go before you always.' The line of I go before you always resonated within me deeply. That, as head of our family, this was the last earthly job he had to do for us.

Because now I have no fears of dying. It will be with joy of knowing I can be eight years old again, running to him, jumping high into his arms, being bear-hugged and just filled with that joy of 'Hello Daddy!'

My father and I were our own little peas in a pod. We looked very alike and had quite similar personalities, passionate and proud. When he passed over, I began to feel very much like him, pragmatic, practical. There's a job to be done, just do it, overtaking me. I found myself gently getting out of bed at 7.30 a.m. to exercise as he did daily. I was a lover of the snooze button. My sister accidentally cut my hair too short. Now by male standards, I had a fine head of hair – about the only thing my father lamented was his loss of hair. I had to brylcream it now too just as he did. I was told that heaven is the soul of a parent alive in a child. I had never felt so emotionally balanced as I did after his passing. I guess in a very short space of time, I had found that heaven on earth with my Dad. He resides within me now and it's a very comfortable place. I'm allowed at times to be the old emotional me, but the over indulgence of loss, the mantle of mourning that etched my heart for a decade, has left my heart. It did not bring me joy. I would see that as Daddy being happy in heaven and wanting us to be happy here too.

Grief, as birth, is a unique experience for all. There is no easy labour, there is no easy death. What we all have at any one time is the power of choice, how we choose to live.

I choose life as Daddy did. I choose to live and to honour any sadness I feel in any day. I experienced great love from my father. As in physics, for every action there is an equal but opposite reaction. So too with great love on earth (how love is quantified I do not know), there is equal but opposite sadness of that earthly love. That too I just accept. I have no desire to resist. It just is as it is. It's life. I accept the sadness that accompanies death. I have no desire to resist or deny it as that to me would be to deny how much I loved my Dad.

My father lived out his story of cancer and now I will live out my story of grief. A bit like him, in my own way. I have not felt any stages of grief, maybe in his illness I grieved his life before he passed. I don't think that there is a correct way to be. I think I'll just be me.

In conclusion, my father to me was a great man, a wonderful man, a brave man, a very proud Kerryman whom I adored with all my heart. He was my rock for always in my life. He always remained faithfully by my side, a lot of the time when I didn't deserve it but I received his unconditional love in abundance always, in spite of my imperfections. He was in essence, my everything and the gratitude I feel to have been worthy of his love for all my life is immense.

Ar dheis Dé go raibh anam dílis m'athair go deo agus ionam don tamall gearr a mhairfidh mé ar an saol seo.

The Lid Lifter

My earliest vivid memory of my father is holding his hand above my head as we walked up toward Clondalkin village, at a stride ratio of about fifteen of mine to one of his. Lagging behind, like a floppy water-skier, begging him to slow down. His hand was so big that half my arm seemed to disappear within its clasp. That was through the eyes of a four-year-old, however in reality they were still massive and, as the song goes, thundering velvet hands. I would watch how he pressed them together at Mass, I would feel the strength in them as we walked, him holding mine in his, and in the evenings I would sit with Mam and Dad on couch and play, squishing the veins on the back of his hands, watching them refill. I know my brothers and sisters all did the same when they were kids.

I was the youngest, by a long shot, of six children. They were all numbered amongst the earls that flew this island in the 1980s in search of work. So, to all intents and purposes, when it came to everyday life growing up in Clondalkin, I was an only child, albeit with five guardian angels fighting my corner from afar. As a result, I had uninterrupted access to both Mam and Dad with very few reasons to rebel, thanks in great part to those guardian angels smoothing the path.

When I started work, Dad wasn't long away from retirement. He was a flexographic printer by trade. We talked about life, family, politics, love, history, the papers, whatever came up. Equally, if there were nothing to say, we'd sit in silence. There was a quiet acceptance, a comfort there. How our relationship was evolving over time would also become a topic of our discussions.

As we grew closer, I fell into the role of 'lid lifter'. A curious naming convention, I'll admit, but an important role nonetheless and a potentially infuriating one for others. The lid lifter is the person who comes along after you have been struggling to open the jam jar and lifts the lid effortlessly. Ultimately, you will claim to have 'loosened the lid' that seemed to come away with such ease. Well, with Dad, I was the lid lifter. The family nicknames for me were Golden balls, Platinum balls and the Oracle. Over the years if Mam grew tired of trying to get Dad to do something, usually regarding his health, she would give me a call to come down and speak with him. I would drop by, put on the kettle, make a pot of coffee and broach the subject. With the lid well and truly loosened, by Mam and others, I was usually able to lift it and get Dad to concede to do whatever needed to be done. These jam jars that required opening could be as important as attending a pain management specialist (for whom he had developed a dislike), as practical as bringing his wheelchair on holidays, or as trivial as the location of a comfy chair in his last days.

Dad got little value from his retirement. He retired in April 1995 and had a pulmonary embolism in the August of 1996. That was the start of it ... and it sure as hell wasn't the end of it. Numerous bouts of cancer in his face and bowel meant he was in constant pain, although for the most part you wouldn't know it. He bore a stoic and graceful temperament, preferring to answer: 'I'm grand' to any enquiry after his wellbeing. The subtext was always: 'Aside from the searing, burning pain in my face, the tinnitus, the failing eye sight and the fact that I have no abdominal wall to speak of ... I'm Grand!'

The last chapter began in early June 2010. My wife, Joyce's father had passed away, in Waterford, at the end of May and both Mam and Dad had travelled for the funeral. Dad held a special place in his heart for Joyce. He admired her qualities, was immensely proud of her achievements and loved her almost as much as I do. After the Mass, Leo was buried in a graveyard on a steep hill and Dad was determined to be by the graveside for Joyce. No one did 'determined' like Aidan Flood, that's for sure. In hindsight he was very unsteady on his feet, but he was there to protect and support her in a way that only he could.

Ultimately, I was the one with Dad the morning he received the news. That was a sad time. Delia was the registrar for the oncology teams that had worked on all of Dad's previous battles with cancer, and as a result, had known Mam and Dad for the last thirteen years. The message was almost as difficult for her to deliver as it was for Dad to receive. He had secondary cancer cells, the prognosis was terminal and the main consideration of the oncology team would be quality of life.

Our hearts sank. This was a message that Dad had expected to hear many times before, but one for which nobody is ever ready. As we spoke with Delia a while longer I held Dad's hand in my own. This time mine enveloped his with ease. Then, in the voice of the little boy I had never met, Dad asked her ... 'If you were in my position, what would you do?' In that moment I wanted to pick him up and carry him home. We would have to wait another few weeks before we could do that.

My final call to 'lift a lid' occurred when Dad came home from the hospital and for the first few days had the full intention of continuing to come downstairs from time to time.

The chair had been provided for him after his previous illness to support his back and make it easier for him to stand up from sitting. It was located in the front room and while it looked like a hospital chair, it was a very comfortable one. If he wasn't in it, I had dibs on it. He refused to have it brought up to the bedroom, preferring to leave it in the front room, for when he went downstairs. It soon became clear that was not going to happen. Eventually, I brought up the subject with him, used the same arguments, condemning the crappy wicker chair as uncomfortable and ... 'Wouldn't it be better to have the comfy chair up here, be comfortable, and have me bring it downstairs when the whim takes you to venture down.' Sure enough, he conceded and I brought the chair up, then and there. My sister, Jean, took some lovely photos of Mam, Dad and herself, with Dad sitting in that chair in the bedroom, days before he passed away.

My point is this, when Dad died, that role of lid lifter, Oracle, Golden balls, went with him and I found this difficult to reconcile. To tell the truth, I still do.

Who am I now? What purpose do I serve?

Then, when I looked deeper, I saw that this role had been developed on the foundation of our mutual investment in the relationship. Many long chats, many opinions shared and just as many argued. We had built a respect for each other and each revered and sought the others' opinions and advice. We were best friends first and foremost.

Initially this made it even worse. Not only had I lost my father, my role model and a best friend, I had also lost my mentor. Then I recognised that as well as highlighting my loss, this realisation revealed what we had built. There was a subtlety to our communication. Things were spoken and understood in our silences and there was an abundance of silence in our communications now. I set about understanding what was being said in these silences. It took a while, but once I tuned in I could really hear his advice and feel his presence. That gave me a huge sense of connection and protection.

Song had been an integral part of our upbringing and of Mam and Dad's relationship. After all it had been through music they had met for the first time. At 12.30 a.m. on the 26 July 2010, Mam did something that, until then, for her, had been unthinkable. She gave Dad permission to go. Then lay by his side and started to sing. It was a beautiful moment that I will remember always. Everyone was there, by that I mean all my brothers and sisters, and we were singing. Singing whatever came into Mam's head, the songs we knew that is. Suggesting one or two as the song titles came to us. Watching our fathers face change. Noticing his breath fail slowly and ultimately witnessing his surrender to the next phase.

In that moment his face changed again. The pain was gone and had been replaced with an acceptance. A wonder. An anticipation of what was around the next corner. A trust and grace was etched there and that gave me a great sense of comfort. He knew there was more and was excited about experiencing it.

It is said that, in death, life has changed, not ended. This was the moment that Dad's life started to change and, with it, all of the relationships he had forged with those inside the room and out. The singing had continued for an hour or so. The last two songs we sang for him were, 'Can't help loving that man of mine' and 'Go to sleep my little drummer boy', the latter being the soundtrack to our ultimate farewell.

It was a happy, sad, gorgeous, devastating, encouraging, wonderful moment that I will be hard pressed to equal in my lifetime. I am just blessed to have been there. I like the thought that in those last moments, the hands whose veins we'd squished, that had provided so much protection and encouragement for us all, felt protected and encouraged, safe in the cradle of the hands they had nurtured.

Seven months on and some observations have slowly dawned on me. Like, never underestimate the physical impact that emotional turmoil yields. It exhausts! Or the fact that grief heeds no schedule but it's own. However, if I were to offer only one piece of advice, it would be: to cry when you want to cry, laugh when you want to laugh. Because when a loved one passes away, you will spend most of your time doing both, simultaneously.

Mr Africa – Living Through Me

His love for Africa is what earned him the name Mr Africa. He was a very smart, intelligent and kind man who believed in humanity and his big laughter always brought warmth into people's lives. That was my father, Mr Africa Cephas Munanairi, a Zimbabwean, who had been sent to exile and found himself in Kenya. He loved books and was well-read with over 6,000 copies of books stored in his home library and he knew each book by heart. He educated many people from poor backgrounds, not only did he sponsor their education; he also taught them things that they would never learn in classrooms. He was well-travelled all over the world, Europe, the Middle East, Asia, America and Canada. By the time of his death, he was in the process of completing a book entitled *Man as his own author*, which unfortunately never came to be.

Mr Cephas Munanairi was the founder of the Kenya Voluntary Development Association. He also worked closely with UNESCO and OAU (Organization of African Unity), among others, and was a member of several organisations internationally.

My father and I were very close mainly because of our resemblance, or just of the fact that we shared the same personality. We shared special memorable moments together; we travelled, cooked, laughed and joked together. He made it so easy to live with other people and taught me the values of life. My father and mother remain my biggest heroes in my life. The greatest lesson he taught me was persistence and perseverance while the greatest gift he gave me was the humbling attribute of appreciation of all human kind regardless of their creed, colour and status. These are the lessons that apply in almost every day of my life, thanks to him. I always looked up to him to solve all the problems in the world. When things were thick, he would always laugh and say: '*Africa, kuna mambo*' meaning, 'Africa has things going'. He was always a cheerful man full of life even when he was angry. He never let it show, it's only those who knew him who could tell that he was angry.

Back in 1992, I noticed that my father's health was not good. This did not worry me much because I thought that, just like any human being, he had contracted an infection on his leg. This was not to be, after several visits to the hospital for medication. Unfortunately, the tests showed nothing which was very strange. He decided to seek help in Germany while on a business trip. Again his results were negative of all the tests that were carried out. This mysterious disease was taking my father away bit by bit. His persistence and perseverance to work and to walk long distances in his work, is something that he will forever be remembered for. He gave service to humanity for the entire period while under great pain without giving up or losing hope. Although gone, his legacy lives strong and most people are reminded of him in their deeds and achievements. He was a great man, a true hero and true crusader for humanity. He believed in the strength of Africa to overcome their problems.

The situation with his leg got worse in late 1993 and it started discharging fluids as though the leg was rotten. This made his life very uncomfortable and impossible for him to gain accessibility in the hotels and other service industry. It was during this time when one lady (God rest her soul) had come to my dad's office to see his secretary who had a vision about him. According to her vision, my dad was very sick and his illness would not be treated by 'doctors'. She further said that his illness had been as a result of bewitching, that's why whenever he went to the hospital he could not be treated.

In July 1994, my dad had become relatively weak from the pain and the discharges. Amazingly, he worked faithfully and addressed the community highlighting the importance of independence against dependency. He had for a long time championed for Africans to create independence in their minds, thoughts and actions. That was the last speech that he delivered.

Back at school, St Martha's Girls High School was a Catholic school with strict rules and every morning we had to attend Mass. I had been having very strange nightmares until I lost concentration in class. I definitely knew that something was not right about my father, yet I could not find out what. One evening I plotted with my friend Gladys Miraba to sneak out of the school to make phone calls home. On this morning as fate had it, my dad had placed the telephone receiver off the hook and so could not get through. On the other hand, some of the girls had sneaked out to go for a disco in the night. Therefore, while coming back, the security man caught us up and that's how we got expelled three months before sitting for our final national examinations. I tried to explain to the Headmistress urging her to call my dad that he was not feeling well, but she would not hear of it.

I did not feel remorseful about the expulsion, I was happy to go home. This astonished the Headmistress very much but later on, she came to feel very sorry about it. My school was eight hours away and thus I always took a night bus. When I got home that morning, my dad opened the door and, with one look at him, I knew he was very sick. He had worn his browned dotted gown. Just like in my dreams, my dad was not in good shape but he kept his smile. He was so kind to me, asking me what was the matter. As I explained to him my dreams and worries, his frail body told it all.

I nursed my dad while at home at the same time doing my studies. I would cook for him, clean his leg and talk to him. He would always tell me stories and appreciate my company. He loved me very much to a point where he didn't want me to see him in pain. He would always tell me something to make me laugh but I knew he was in pain.

In his final days, he lost his appetite and finally his sight. This was a major blow for a man who loved to read so much. I was so traumatised for him and kept my strong spirit going just for him. When my relatives flew in from Zimbabwe, I remember crying in the bathroom sink under the running water. I could not hold it any longer. This is the point when I realised that my father was really suffering. He did not want to be flown to Zimbabwe. He kept on saying if he was flown the plane would crash. Every night, I would have nightmares about him. One particular nightmare was very vivid and specific. A voice said: 'Mr Munanairi going to Zimbabwe will be very difficult.' That morning I told my mum and brother and they both dismissed me. By that time, my father was furious about his departure to Zimbabwe and was not speaking to anyone.

The trip was finalised towards the end of September. Everyone was leaving except for me because of my upcoming examinations. I was to remain behind. That morning, we left for the airport and I cried all the way. When we got there, my dad's leg started bleeding and we were asked to go to the hospital, so the flight was cancelled. We took him to the hospital and they administered more valium and dressed his leg after which we went back home. I was happy to have him around. Two days later, the entourage left for the airport, this time their bags made it through but they were unable to leave because my brother did not have a return ticket, so again they were sent back home and I was very happy. Some people thought it was my entire fault because I kept on crying every time we drove to the airport. On the last day, I was warned sternly to let my dad go and not cry because if I did he would never go. So I tried to hold myself together to the airport, kept calm until they all boarded a flight and I went to the waving bay and saw him in a wheel chair. When the plane reached the sky, I started crying and that was the last time I saw my father alive. A week later a telegram arrived that he had passed. He passed on 2 October 1994. On that day, I had a dream of him talking to me and he was in good form and I was so happy because he was healed. My father was gone forever which sometimes I still find very hard to believe. I sometimes feel as though he had travelled and he would be back someday.

The healing process has remained the most difficult thing for me because I never attended his burial. He passed on and a week later I had to sit for the examination. I was still in shock and didn't realise the intensity when I went back to school. The entire staff were shocked and could not understand how I had figured out about my dad. I will forever remain thankful for the last moments we shared with him. He gave me an insight into life that I will pass on to my children and others. My mother was a very strong pillar for my healing, she was there, gave us everything we needed, most of all emotional support.

The most important lesson has been to appreciate the time we shared and the values he passed to me. Although it is difficult, I have learnt to let him live through me and acknowledge his departure because his work on this earth is done. He brought me into this world, gave me the best of everything and left me with the best legacy of his wisdom and knowledge through education. I thank you Dad and think of you often.

Succisa Virescit
(Cut down, it grows up stronger again)

I put the receiver back down on the cradle, sat back in my chair and exhaled. It, quite literally, was the call I had been dreading for more than four years. My father had said it matter-of-factly and without adornment: 'Geoff, hello, it's your father. I think you better come home.'

It was a simple sentence, but it carried with it all the bad news of someone losing a four year battle with cancer; my mother was going to die. I stood up in my little corner cubicle, looked around at the boxes of people and glass and flickering screens and, not knowing quite what to do, walked to the refuge of that floor's bathroom. I don't remember the walk there, but I found myself sitting with my head in my hands and I felt absolutely nothing. I don't remember exactly what I said to the people in my office, I don't remember how I got back from Boston to New York, whether I took the train or drove. Mostly what I remember is feeling nothing. I got home late and the house was empty. I decided to take the train into the hospital the next morning and face up to what was coming. I walked upstairs, lay down on my parents' bed, and fell into a fitful sleep.

When I woke up I forgot for that first second why I was there and what was going on. Then it came rushing in all at once and I felt all my emotions rushing up and I thought I might cry from the shock of it. Then I felt nothing but panic that I might have slept all day and people were trying to reach me and I had missed everything. I don't remember driving to the train with my Aunt Mary.

I don't remember getting there, but we arrived at St Vincent's Hospital in New York sometime after noon. We walked into the hallway and I could see bright lights shining on the white hospital walls and highlighting the neutral colours of the floors and doors. I saw my Aunt Terry and my sister Jane standing nervous and exhausted outside the room. They looked up and saw me and at once were relieved and sad. It was an instantaneous process I would come to know well over the next six hours as each new person came. I hesitated for just one second outside the door and inhaled deeply and sharp at the same time. I saw my mom, the covers were halfway up with a few tubes, one down her throat and her eyes were closed. My brothers and sisters were around the bed and crying. My father I saw looked exhausted and was also crying. I was instantly angry, why was she sedated? I wanted to talk to her, I wanted to see her eyes, have her see mine. I wanted to comfort her while she went through this, I wanted her to comfort me as I went through this. No, the nurse said, they knew it didn't work, it was too hard on the patient and the family. What did she know about what I needed or my mother needed? I said nothing and hugged some of the people around me, I don't remember exactly who.

I walked over to the bed and picked up her hands and I could literally feel the life coming and going in the palm of my mom's hands, and I snapped back to reality with a sudden jerk. I walked around and numbly tried to comfort my siblings. 'She's waiting for Jimmy to get here ...', I heard my Aunt Terry blurt out, though I realised I had heard the end of the conversation and could not remember what came before it. Then suddenly a few things happened – I can't remember what – just all of a sudden we were all asked to leave the room by several nurses, it was all a blur.

Then they came out and said just the immediate family could come back in. I hesitated just outside the door, took a deep breath and walked in. This time the covers were all the way up, all the tubes were gone except the detached trachea tube, and someone thoughtful had put a little teddy bear by her shoulder. I sat down on the ratty chair and pulled it up to the bed, I took my mom's hand and I pulled it up to my forehead and I wept uncontrollably. I remember I could feel the tears just coming out of my body in great big drops without any control by me. I could feel them pouring through my hands and collecting on the floor. I thought about driving to my grandmother's house in the summertime and the dappled light coming through the window, while we listened to *Summer Breeze* on the radio. I thought about learning how to dive in our pool, I thought about riding the Scrambler in between my two parents when I was very small, I thought about all the times when I was bad, and I felt it all so suddenly, that it took my breath away and I could not possibly imagine how it was going to be to live without this person in my life.

The next hours and days passed in a whirl of flowers and wakes and planning speeches and sandwiches and frozen lasagna and trying to make other people feel better. Then trying to find someone who would say hello without giving that look of pain as they said hello, then trying to find someone who would stop asking me how I was or how my family was doing. I had agreed at some point to give one of the eulogies, and was really struggling to put my thoughts down on paper. I had really wanted to do it, so I was glad when they asked me to. I even thought it my duty as the eldest.

Oh my God, the eldest of eight children, I forgot. What would these little kids do? My mom had been pregnant with Christine when she was first diagnosed. The doctors had recommended termination of the pregnancy when the tumour went malignant, but my mom had refused. Now Christine would grow up without any mother, my mother.

When it was time to get ready for the actual funeral and eulogy, I felt nothing. My brother Ted asked me if I was ready. I, wanting to be big for everyone, answered very cocksure that I was fine. Public speaking is easy for me. 'Well if you have any trouble I can come up and say ... ' I cut him off and assured him it wouldn't be necessary. I wrote my speech in the three minute ride to the church. Aunt Terry typed hers.

I got two sentences in and predictably thought of my brother and choked up with tears. Ted quite gamely got up and tried to talk about my mom for a few minutes, which gave me the full time to laugh and recover and then go on with my speech. Baby Christine was very annoyed that I had cried and interrupted the important proceedings. We all then marched out with everyone looking at us and walked over to the graveyard for the burial.

We went through the formal part of the proceedings and then I waited for everyone to leave.

My cousins Steven and Jimmy hung back with me and we all had some Jamesons I had brought along in an attempt to emulate my grandfather's 'wee drop at the grave' story, much to his delight I found out later.

It would be three more years before I felt normal. As I look back now, I am amazed at what I remember, and even more amazed about what I don't remember. This person had had the most profound effect on me, more than any person on earth, yet I don't think of her everyday anymore. I miss my Mom, and I am glad I knew her. I remember all the good things, and all the bad. It does not hurt me anymore. I sometimes feel guilty about that but now I have new things to do. Will I have enough money, will I be happy at my job, will I be a good husband, will I be a good parent, will I be good enough? I think about all of the things I got to talk to her about, all of the things that I want to talk about now, and I know that I have been cheated. Every once in awhile it will sneak up and wash over me all at once, and I feel everything; and I know for sure that I don't ever want to feel nothing again.

His Presence Is Beside Me Always

I find this very difficult to do, partly I am afraid or maybe I never really dealt with or experienced a full healing from the time of my Dad's death. Maybe it's well and truly time that I did.

My Dad was born on the 23 March 1906 and named Frederick Usher Sparkes. He passed away on 4 August 1993. He was in his eighty-eighth year.

My Dad was the best father one could ever have. He was my mentor, my teacher, my inspiration and my best friend. He was a dairy farmer and a gardener, a loving and tender man to a child, where a healing kiss on my cut knee would stop the tears; a sensitive man who cried with jubilant emotion on my school prize day when I received an award in the Children's Caltex Art competition. My Dad was one with the earth, knew each of the seasons and all that nature produces. A gentle man and a thinker, a man who was shy, a creative man who loved growing his vegetables and flowers, milked his cows by hand and gave each one of them names which I think they understood.

He taught me all that I know about gardening and I try to recall it as I look after my small patch. To this day I can hear his voice softly instructing me, it's as if his presence is beside me. I remember when I was six years old, having my own little part of the garden for my self, I too would plant my vegetable seeds and bulbs and care for them just like my Dad. I too smelt the earth and watched them grow. There is nothing to replace the glow of satisfaction when you eat your own supplies.

My Dad lived to a great age of eighty-seven years, only in the latter two years of his life did his body really begin to show its age. Out walking the wind would slow his breath and require him to take a breather. His garden became a couple of tubs which I would place on the patio table and together we would plant the 'annuals'. Then suddenly it was all gone. I remember the pain and the sorrow I felt in my chest when the dreaded phone call came to tell me he had passed into the next world, it was as if the very breath was taken from me too.

The day of his funeral was a typical Irish summers' day, heavy cloud, showers and glimpses of sunshine. As he was laid to rest I can recall a brightness appearing in the atmosphere, as if to reassure me he was now amongst the heavens and at one with his maker. My Dad was a believer in God and the resurrection of Jesus Christ. He used to often say as he walked through the garden: 'Only the hand of God can create such beauty.' This assurance has stayed with me all through my life.

The hardest time was the day my Mum and I cleared out his personal things, his clothes and his shoes. I remember looking at his brown leather shoes, he always wore leather as it was kinder to his feet, seeing the indentations where his toes would have been it was as if his feet were still in them and I cried. I cried again when my Mum handed me his purse in which he kept his coins, I counted them and thought there is not much here, I still have that purse hidden among my personal things. I kept a jumper which he regularly wore because it had his smell on it. I only parted with it recently, it went into the charity bag. My hope is that the person who wears it will feel warm and comfortable in it too.

I don't know if my grieving journey is ever over, even in a crowded street when I catch a glimpse of a man who reminds me of my father especially the head part, I get quite a shock. Up to his death he had a thick head of white hair, he was always proud of it, he often said, he got value for money at the barber shop.

In the eons of time we only have a short life here on earth and quoting from *Prayers of Life* by Michel Quoist: 'For a Christian, death does not exist, or, rather it is only a starting point and not an end', and as St Thérèse of Lisièux, on her death bed, murmured: I am not dying, I am entering into life.'

Through all your sadness I am grateful for this opportunity to recall the wonderful times Dad and I had together and to grieve some more and some more.

The Swaying Barley Stalks

I was seventeen at the time, I shut down the big, noisy harvester out in the middle of a barley field. The sky was full of fluffy clouds lazily floating by, close enough to reach, you know what I mean. I just needed to be quiet; everything of the past couple of months was really confusing, I was not able to connect all the dots. Nobody to really talk to, people just take things for granted. But for me, I thought how naïve. Not me, I needed more, I was about to burst.

I was hoping beyond hope to see the Blue Dodge Pickup coming across the fields to bring me a snack and to check up on me, to see how I was doing with the harvesting, I was sure it would come. It didn't …

Time, just to reflect. As I lay there, the wind causing the barley stalks heavy with grain to sway back and forth in concert, I marvelled how the world for those few moments seemed peaceful, almost surreal. The crop was bountiful, it was going to be a good year, easily remembering the great depression and the postwar years, things were really bleak then, but now finally we were going to make it.

Back to work, more work, decisions, on how to keep over two thousand acres of hay and seed crops on to market, and not least of all taking care of the large pig operation and my small black Angus heifers that I bought one at a time, so very carefully with my savings.

I had quit school in the spring of my junior year to put my full time into the operation. I had to move on. With all this preoccupation, I was not hearing the whispers behind my back. My mother, in her early thirties, was devastated, unable to cope with the stress of the preceding events. I did not pay attention, I had to keep moving on, tending the ranch as best I knew how.

I was to be the farmer's kid for the rest of my life. I did not have a college prep course under my belt, why should I? It was the early fifties, post WWII, everything was sweet, 'Happy Days'.

179

I remember the day when I was about six or seven that my dad brought home a beautiful shiny red bike. Bolted to the top tube, a sign that read, Johnny Oakes Special. I could see that great grin, curly red hair parted slightly on the left side. I never saw him without a grin, even when things were tough financially, he was never without it. What character, physically trim, determined and always ready to help someone in need. I saw that exhibited numerous times, and it always left me wondering. The bike facilitated my being able to carry my brown eggs to market every Saturday, balancing a wire basket on the handlebar. Never crashed or broke an egg.

One day, during my junior year of high school, I was called out of class and given the instruction to, 'Go home immediately'. There I met my mother and our family doctor, Dr Andrews was his name. There had been an accident on the ranch, a tractor had tipped over on the Levy. Before we got to the site, a car met us and said it was too late. That event started a whole chain reaction of events that would change my life and attitude, 'I thought forever'. That night I had to identify the body, the last time I saw that great smile, and curly red hair parted slightly on the left side.

Slowly, the anger welled up: unfair, I needed help. But there was not really anyone that knew how to help me. There were no classes for grieving kids, but of course at that time I didn't know what that meant anyway. Family members came and went, and I just held it in.

Somehow, another story for another time, I did make it to college with a scholarship, not academic but sports.

I did not know what it was but anger was packed deep inside my core. It came out in different ways, defiance: risk-taking and directed towards others. If not verbally, then physically. The real paradox was that I had this deep desire to help others who were down and out. I did not know how to reconcile these two very different sets of emotions that were rooted inside me. The desire to help the underdog was modelled early in my childhood.

There was a need in my life for someone that I could trust, one who would speak the truth, both spiritually and emotionally. Someone who honestly cares, listens and who does not have the pat answer to every issue of life. That benefit came to me, but not until I was a mature man. So many years have passed. Don't wait, reach now.

I'll never forget the last broad smile, curly red hair parted on the left side, broad square chin, ruddy face and trim athletic body, as I identified his body at the mortuary. Would I ever be the farmer's kid again, on a bike for Johnny Oakes Special?

STORY WRITTEN BY KAREN BENZ

Gifts in Times of Sorrow

My dad was adventurous, giving, entrepreneurial and creative. He and my mom made sure we went camping every summer and skiing every winter, regardless of our family's financial situation. One summer when I was thirteen, we lived on the boardwalk of Bonnet Shores Beach Club in a tiny apartment – all eight of us – while my dad and his friend managed the beach club. Talk about a 'dream summer'!

He was a skilled craftsman, making most of the furniture in his home. He loved to carve birds and make Shaker boxes. He was a legendary skier and loved playing hockey with his brother, Don. He was also a deeply religious and faithful man.

When he turned sixty, his health began to fail. He needed heart surgery, and he was diagnosed with COPD (chronic obstructive pulmonary disease) and emphysema. At the age of eighty-two, in the last year of his life, he required oxygen. He and my mom began to make plans. Being the extraordinary pragmatists they were, they planned for renovations to the house – all sorts of projects my dad loved to be involved in. The projects were just about completed when he was admitted to the hospital in mid-December of 2010.

After five days in the critical care unit at the hospital, a palliative care physician came to talk with us. He said my dad would be more comfortable at the hospice care facility. So, this was the end. Dad, being a man of faith, had accepted his time on earth was about to end. As a family, our grieving process had begun.

I believe that in times of sorrow and pain, there are gifts as well. Dad had the opportunity to say goodbye to family and close friends. We, children and grandchildren, were all able to celebrate his last Christmas and it was beautiful.

All of the children were able to have time with dad to have closure – he wanted to tell us how much we have meant to him in his life. I told him that I was sorry for any grief I caused him growing up, but I had realised something over the years: that I

182

was just like him, stubborn, tenacious, adventurous, giving and entrepreneurial. He agreed and told me I needed to 'find my own star'. That conversation is one I will cherish for the rest of my life.

In the end, he wanted to die at home. We gathered around his bed and held his hands. I stroked his face. Mom told him he could let go. I remember feeling, in that moment, so strong and so sure that this was the time he wanted to go. When it was over, we all kissed him and then clung to one another, not believing it was over.

I still miss him every day. I keep his memory and spirit alive by talking about him with my kids and family. My mom is doing well, which helps all of us. But I still miss him. My grieving journey has just begun – or so it feels.

What I've learned throughout this entire process is:

- Everyone grieves in their own way, at their own pace, and expresses it differently. Therefore, I try not to judge anyone else on how they grieve, based on my own process.
- I must be patient with my grief. It's a process, and it will take time. It takes however long it takes.
- When the grief comes, I have to let the feelings wash over me, like a wave because I know it will pass.

I had a professional biographer interview my dad and film it just two months before he died. As a result, we each have an oral history of dad's life on DVD. We had no idea it would be such a gift. I haven't been able to watch it yet. When I do watch it, I know my healing will have truly begun.

The Strength Losing My Parents Brings

Losing a parent at a young age creates a life challenge that can never be fully understood or overcome. It can devastate or strengthen as with many other things God throws at us in life. I lost my dad at age two and my mother at age seventeen. It was a tough, rocky road and in the end I've led a very successful life. I commanded a US Navy Submarine, ran a $350 million dollar company, and now run a successful business of my own with a great family backing me up.

These losses are the core of much of the good and bad in my life. In sharing my story, I hope you will see the strength which losing a parent early can bring, and learn from the mistakes I made.

The Early Years

My dad was killed in a Navy accident when I was just two. His ship, the *USS Hobson* was cut in half by the aircraft carrier *USS Wasp* and sunk in four minutes losing 176 young sailors.

From the start, my extended family of aunts, uncles, and grandparents was so very supportive. There is no doubt that I felt their love and it sustained me for the rest of my life. There is a powerful lesson there for families and friends: never underestimate the lifetime gift you will give by supporting a grieving family with young kids suddenly missing a parent.

Of course, being only two when my dad was killed, I never knew how it felt to be held by him, what his face looked like from my own memory, or how it felt to learn a lesson from him at first-hand. At first, I never really 'noticed' I was different, but as I grew it became obvious the other kids with dads had a real advantage. I'd get invited with friends and their dads for small things, but when the really special times came I'd be left out. That hurt and eventually I started to build up resentment at losing my dad so early.

Another theory I have about losing a parent at such a young age is you never complete the grieving process. At two, those emotions were not mature enough to even understand, much less process, grief. As I did mature, there was no structure to support the traditional grieving process; it just went on and on.

The New Family

At age seven, my mother remarried. My new family had five kids with me right in the middle age-wise. Now just think about that, going from an only child, well cared for by family and friends, to the middle child in a family of eight. And, by the way, we promptly moved from our home in Charleston SC to California with no family and no friends. Ouch, that hurt.

My view of the world as a loving, nurturing place quickly disappeared like water into sand. I was in a fend-for-yourself world. I drew up a wall around myself and took care of number one. My view of the world had changed to a place that can take away everything in a flash of light. My wall approach got me through; a star in the band, a high school diploma, a Navy scholarship to college, and a toughness that gives me the stamina to hang in there when everything around me is falling apart.

I can't fault my Mother; she was a great woman with a huge heart. She came from a family of nine kids, so I'm sure in her world the new big family was going to be a positive move for us. Plus, she was in love and deserved a great new life after suffering what she had lost too. It must have all made sense at the time, the perfect plan. If there's a lesson there, I'd say to single moms and dads, go slowly and *really* think through those new family decisions. And a side note, it sure would have been nice if she had asked me – yes even a seven-year-old! I'd have probably said 'go for it' and would have maybe taken a different approach in my behavior.

The 'Second' Loss

The marriage and new family was as big a disaster for my Mom as it was for me. She was suddenly Mom to six kids who brought their own set of single parent problems to the table. I was not much help. I still demanded a lot of attention, more like an only child than a middle-child for sure. I disliked my step-dad and as time grew, I more and more resented the fact that he pretended to be my dad. It just never clicked with us.

My mother's marriage gradually deteriorated to a perpetual state of separation. I was back to being an only child, it was during my last two years of high school. Actually in those times, things were looking up again. I had some spectacular friends in high school. I went to visit my mom and real dad's families in North Carolina for several weeks each summer. Life was good and I was turning the corner.

As I entered my senior year of high school, at age sixteen, my mom started having a lot of medical problems. She had a bad back, several surgeries, and was in and out of the hospital. My step-dad would pop back in once in a while from Texas. In the spring of my senior year, I learned my mom had cancer. My last two months of school were ones of great joy from graduating and knowing I had a full Navy scholarship to college and pure terror as I gradually learned my mom was going to die.

My mom attended my high school graduation on a stretcher in the back of the auditorium. Two weeks later she passed away gently in the Charleston Naval Hospital, just moments after I'd left her side. We buried her next to my real dad in North Carolina. I went to the service alone and drove myself to the graveside. I was totally on my own. I knew it and it sucked!

Being the tough guy I was, at seventeen, I hired a lawyer, had an aunt and uncle appointed my guardian and negotiated a fair settlement over my mom's estate with my step-dad. There is some chance he wasn't the ogre I make him out to be. I'll never know. I got the house, worth $18,000 that saw me through college and into the Navy. I made it through that summer with high school friends at my side almost every day. Thank God for those men, several of whom are still great friends today. I fell back on my extended family too, playing golf with my uncles in North Carolina and sailing with my paternal grandfather who loved me like the son he had lost early too.

The College Dip

College is where the proverbial shit hit the fan for me. I made it through the first semester with solid B grades in aerospace engineering. To get that scholarship, I'd gone eight hours away to college with zero friends and zero family support.

I fell right in with the heavy drinking crowd. They were great fellows and we had a ton of fun. We would take late night car trips all over the south, returning to campus only having missed a few classes. My grades slipped and I'd found an emotional crutch that was dragging me down, not holding me up.

Inside, I knew I was going to be somebody, a successful member of society. I never gave up, thanks to the first loss of my dad. I knew I'd survive, I could do it, and nothing was going to stop me. In the end, the same Navy that took my dad early gave me my life back with discipline, opportunity, and community. I stopped drinking so heavily, started making the Dean's List, shifted my studies to Nuclear and Mechanical Engineering. I was accepted as an officer in the Navy's prestigious Nuclear Powered Submarine Program. In four short years I'd gone from hopelessly adrift to focused and successful.

The Lingering Fear

My major fear, in my twenties and thirties, was about living a short life. With my dad gone at twenty-nine and my mom at forty-four, I figured anything past thirty-five was gravy for me. I lived that way: drinking too much, driving my career at the expense of family, and never letting anyone get too close.

After about forty, I realised that I'd better re-think my approach to life. That maybe a better plan was to 'live each day as though I was going to live to be ninety, yet know I might not live until tomorrow'. It's given me a great balance to have fun, take risks, and yet still avoid the excesses that can bring you down.

The Positives

My strength of perseverance is a trait that I cherish more than any other. It keeps me going through other losses, business downturns, and my own physical challenges of aging. I learned early what Franklin D. Roosevelt said about perseverance: 'When you come to the end of your rope, tie a knot and hang on.'

Being a better parent is a clear result of losing one early. Any man or woman who knows that loss also knows how precious the role of a parent is to a child and gives that special care and attention. Today I'm blessed with a great family, a loving wife and a teenage son who is my best friend. He's a great young man who will make some superb contributions to society. His grandparents would be so proud of him. For anyone wondering how losing a parent early will impact you as an adult, take this away: you will be a great parent.

The last of the top positives is that I do live each day with a zest for life. For some that comes late in life, or not at all. They never appreciate how truly precious and tenuous life really is. It's hard to see at first, but knowing about our own mortality early on is a powerful lesson. All great religions teach this lesson, but reading it in a book is nothing like living it first-hand when you are a child.

If I Could Only Have Changed These Things

Today you have the option of *real* medical help in the form of psychotherapy. Of course, at two years old being on the couch with a therapist would not have done much good. However, I have to say that at seven, again at fifteen, and surely after I lost my mom at seventeen, there were perfect opportunities to get some real help. In my case I never talked to a professional, or anyone else for that matter, about my losses until in marriage counselling decades later. Get help for your kids and for yourself.

Use your spiritual strength. Spirituality is built around the message of death, mortality, and eternal life. Use the strength in these lessons. In my case, I was raised with a strong Christian spirituality. I remember one church service right after my mom's death where the pastor made a strong pitch to get more tithing to pave the parking lot. I took the negative from that and didn't go back to church for many years, a serious mistake. If only someone had led me back and steadied me as I re-learned my spiritual strength, I'm convinced my mental health would have recovered in a fraction of the time.

Bad choices are easy to make in your grief at a young age. Bad friends over good, alcohol over exercise, car trips over studies; these are just a few of my decisions that went wrong. They are way too easy to make and impossible to see for yourself at the time. I know that there were times when my aunts and uncles knew I was screwing up and said nothing. They loved me so much and felt so sorry for me that they didn't speak up. Now I wish they had taken me to the wood shed and given me a good spanking. Maybe, just maybe, it would have sped me on my road to recovery.

Conclusion

If you are the son or daughter who lost a parent early, take heart! There will be tough times, you will get down, you will lose your way, but that loss will strengthen and empower you in ways you can't appreciate now. Let those who love you help you. Recognise that this won't 'just go away', you will have to face it every single day for the rest of your life. How you react to that reality, whether you face it head-on or run for cover will determine the outcome.

My advice is to 'do all you can do' every day. If the day is getting you down, see it and be down. Let it flow through you, grieve with it, handle it without the crutches of alcohol or drugs. When the days are great, enjoy them and rejoice but don't get complacent. Give thanks to those helping you, listen to them, and grow. Know that there will be ups and downs. Find your strengths and let your parent's loss build on those strengths. Make them proud and make yourself proud too.

Fly Away, Jean

I first met Jean Dinwoodie, my future mother-in-law, in a lovely senior living facility in Pennsylvania. Jean and her husband, who had passed away six years before, had retired there.

My fiancé, Don Dinwoodie, and I were driving a U-Haul truck from Massachusetts to Colorado and stopped on the way to visit for a few days. We joined Jean for a candlelit dinner in her elegant dining room with her long-time friends – also residents.

Then I heard the 'stories' – ones that I would hear repeated for nine years to come. Jean had a form of dementia and one of her coping mechanisms was to stick with what she knew: stories mostly from her childhood. I loved those stories and it got to be fun to anticipate and say the stories in my head as Jean was speaking them. Word-for-word, because she never waivered from the original version. Jean was a delight – always upbeat and rarely complaining.

Jean, Don and I had our fun routine. We went shopping. Every outing included chocolate ice-cream from the Strasburg Country Store and Creamery, a store from the 1700s era. No visit was complete without the stories relating to ice-cream, and lunch at Isaacs for Jean's standard Ruben. Jean always brought half of it back for 'later'.

Jean was in remarkable health. Up until her last year, she walked as if she had places to go and people to see: determined and briskly. I loved it because I like to walk that way. Don, a naturally laid back guy, would hustle to keep up with us.

She always called me 'Dear', so I never really knew if she recognised me or not. Her eyes lit up with what could be interpreted as recognition regardless of who entered the room.

I loved to hear her talk about her beloved Stuart, known to her as 'Dinnie', and to hear the stories. I once said I thought that Don took after his father because he is as remarkable a man as I would hear Dinnie was. I never met him except through the stories. Jean would quietly shake her head and say: 'No. No one is like my Dinnie.'

It occurred to me when Jean was about eighty-eight that we, as a family, could take advantage of an opportunity to celebrate her life while she was still alive, instead of waiting until she had passed on. And what a wonderful event we had. Jean was in her glory – the centre of attention, the queen of the ball, and the matriarch of the family.

In the last year of her life, Jean really slowed down. She was ninety-four. Don got the call to come because her body was shutting down – no one illness – just shutting down.

A couple of days later, I joined Don after they had moved Jean to a hospice facility where the life expectancy was four days.

Jean received only some morphine to ease her experience. She was not given water, which surprised and troubled me. But we were assured that this was the proper thing to do.

I didn't want to leave her. I stayed in her room on the couch for the first night. I didn't want her to be alone – to die alone. The second night, my sister-in-law also stayed.

The following day, Don and I went to the music store and bought some beautiful music including the sound of birds. We played the music throughout the day. We could see that Jean was trying to leave but would jerk back for one more breath of air.

I recited the 23rd Psalm – that deeply grounding statement of faith and love, 'Yea though I walk through the valley of the shadow of death, I shall fear no evil; for thou art with me; thy rod and thy staff, they comfort me … My cup runneth over. Surely goodness and mercy shall follow me all the days of my life and I shall dwell in the house of the Lord forever.'

We were cautioned not to touch Jean because it made it more difficult for her to leave – as if the touch would be interpreted as a plea: 'Don't leave us.'

I heard Don tell Jean what a wonderful job she had done as a mother, wife, citizen, and what a wonderful family she had created. Her job was done and she could go. And, to the sound of birds in the background, I said: 'Fly away, Jean.' And she took her last breath…

That moment was the most spiritual moment of my life at that time. I felt the presence of the spirit that was leaving the shell body. I felt Jean's presence and approval of the process of leaving.

We stayed quiet with her for a while before calling the attendants to initiate the removal of the body. The hardest part was when the funeral home representative came and covered her body to take it away. It was the punctuation at the end of the sentence. I thought, 'It is done'.

There was no grieving for Jean. Just poignant memories of wonderful times with her and a full gratitude for the mother of the man I love so deeply.

I was glad for her release. It was her time...

I chose to speak of Jean's death because I learned so much and because that experience prepared me for the death of my own dear mother four years later when she was ninety-eight years of age.

Except for seeing Jean without water, it was not painful for me, but rather a great privilege that I was part of her final moments on earth – and that I could assist her. I felt a special designated role in doing so.

Don had made the decisions to stop life support for both of his parents and he had survived an older brother. He was in quiet grief and I wanted to support him in whatever way possible.

Thank you, Jean, for the joy you gave me in your life, for your dear son, and for the incredible experience of your passing.

My First Step To Maturity

Like for every kid, 'death' or 'dead' have been scary words for me. What I experienced when I was ten years old has brought me to a different level of maturity. This is the story I would like to share with you.

19 May is an important national day (*bairam*) in my country, Turkey. As Güngör family, we woke up to the morning of 19 May, 1963, with this excitement. As we did each *bairam*, we took phaeton to visit our grandparents together with my mom, dad and two sisters.

My dad and I had been like two close friends, or more like two brothers. We would go around together and he would play with me. Another thing we shared together was when we had fish for a meal: he would bone the fish and clean it; then he would give it to me. On that day, we had red mullet for lunch and he fed me with his hands as usual. Then he went to the city club to meet his friends and I went out to play with my friends in front of our house.

I did not realise how time passed; I heard my sister yelling from the window. She shouted: 'Hasan, come home quickly, our father passed away.' I did not know what that meant. I left my friends reluctantly and went home. When I went in, I saw that my mother and a lot of other people were crying. I wanted to go to the living room. I opened the door. There was something lying on the floor and it was covered with white linen. They did not let me go inside the room. There was something extraordinary in the house. All of our rooms were full of people.

That night, they sent me to my uncle's house. I did not understand what was going on. I kept asking where my father was. And they kept telling me, 'He is dead'. But why? I just had fish from his hands. I was trying hard to understand what death really was.

The next day, they brought me back home. It was crowded as the day before. I was told that we were going to the mosque for

193

the funeral and, having spent his final night in his house as a 'guest', it was going to be 'farewell' to my father in the Muslim way. I had heard of these funerals before, but never attended one and I was scared of the dead. I felt the same fear once more and tried to get away from the house. However, they did not let me. According to our customs, only the facial part of the linen would be opened and we were going to see my father for the last time. This was totally impossible for me. There was no way I could look at a dead person, especially when it was my father.

My sisters were showing the same resistance. An old relative of ours called me and my sisters. She told us that 'this ceremony was a part of life, and that we were going to regret it for the rest of our lives if we did not look at his face and this regret would haunt us for the rest of our lives'. She hugged us and took us near the coffin. She removed the white linen. Meanwhile, I shut my eyes very tight and I was frozen. When I opened my eyes, I saw my father's face. He looked as if he was sleeping. His face looked happy and peaceful. I was surprised. If their faces looked like this, why would we be scared of the dead?

My father's coffin was carried on the shoulders of the men and taken to the mosque. This was the last time I saw my father. His final image in my mind was 'my happily sleeping father'.

When I looked at his face for the last time, another feeling struck me: 'He is gone. I will be responsible for my mother and sisters from now on.' I believe that was the moment that I took the first step into maturity.

Years passed and I grew up. I remember the first funeral I attended after my father's. It was an old relative of ours. I was not scared of the dead anymore and I was able to look at his face because I knew I was going to see a happy face. However, I was very surprised by what I saw. His face did not have a trace of a peaceful sleep or happiness. Following this funeral, I saw many other faces in funerals. Almost none of them looked like my father's.

While experiencing my father's death at an early age, I also learned what death meant. I believe what really matters is the picture that we leave behind with what we do when we are alive, and what expression we have on our face when we are dead.

Coming back to eating fish, yes we did keep on eating fish after my father died. I boned and ate my fish by myself. But every time I still remember the last fish my father had me eat. I remember him and the relationship between us.

Last Lessons

Why her death came as a surprise and found us so unprepared is still a mystery to me. It's not that she hadn't had half a lifetime of illness, heart problems and near death experiences. Even after the massive heart attack, and during the weeks during which there was only 'palliative' care, she was determined to get back to eating as usual and playing bridge. Nothing was going to change. Life would be normal. A minor setback, that's all. Walking, Yes, I will go upstairs; No, I don't want a special diet; This food without salt is terrible, what are you trying to do, kill me?

We had our late afternoon visits and morning chats. It was a morning when she said: 'I think if I have something warm for breakfast I'll feel better, I'll call you back' – and then within minutes, the call: 'Your mother has had a stroke.' 'But, that can't be, I just spoke with her. What? She's what?' And then a day of bedside vigil until everything stopped and my mother's spirit left.

Within hours the calls were placed, plane reservations made, flowers ordered – who knew what to do? The burial, the funeral home, the church, do what the undertaker and priest say. They must know. And so we did as we were told; robots, observers, and somehow it was all done until mom was at the edge of her grave, waiting to be buried. And we left, unsettled, incomplete.

Perhaps we knew so little of what to do because of our good fortune to have no deaths in our family, or perhaps it was because of the family's early misfortunes to have had so many deaths in the past that death could not be part of the conversation of the living. But whatever we didn't know for my mother, we learned in our trials by fire and had an all-too-soon opportunity to use this knowledge: the day my mother was buried we learned that death, in the form of cancer, was coming our way again, and soon.

We knew this news was coming. We just didn't know when. He had been treated for cancer for two years, surgery after surgery, sections and re-sections and stents and more problems.

There were two years of discomfort, pain, tubes and uncertainty. What was certain was the sparkle in his eye, the quick smile, paying some attention to doctors' orders but doing what seemed right for him and always looking forward: the grapes will be pruned, the garden will grow, the boat will be ready, spring tides will bring new life and fishing will be great. All the while hoping: maybe they made a mistake, maybe I will actually eat again.

But after two years my father had used his nine lives and on the day his wife of sixty-three years was buried, death stayed around. But at least this time, death gave us time to show what we had learned from my mother's untimely disappearance. It was on this Valentine's Day that we learned what we feared, the cancer had returned, and it was relentless, untreatable. Soon hospice was with us.

In the nine weeks we had, there was time to talk of faith and family and the future. There was time for tears and laughter, visits, birthdays and celebration. We were together, we made sense of the past and we could plan: we sterilised illness and fear. We had time to get our hands and heads and hearts involved in honoring a life well-lived. We knew more now. I realise as I write that I must thank my mom, for again leading the way and teaching in such an unexpected manner: through leaving first. We now had time to put life and leaving in order so by the time Holy Thursday arrived, the cribbage tournament had been played and a Victor crowned, the vines were trimmed and the tennis balls, fishing gear and cribbage board were ready to take their journey with my dad. With the Man in Black attending, Last Rites were administered, and now my father's spirit was gone as well.

But this time, our newly acquired knowledge helped my father leave. We were present to his presence and his absence, to the people who came to acknowledge him, to the mass that honored his spirit, to the few words attempting to describe a full life, to our own feelings and experience. And my father was not by the edge of the grave when we left, as he was lovingly put to rest with the soil and the sod placed carefully by his grandsons who, in confusion and indignation of their nana's burial, had sought relief from the institutional cemetery guidelines, so they could put their pepe to rest. We left the cemetery that day, sad but aware: mom and dad's voices quiet, bodies at rest, spirits released, the cycles complete, children and grandchildren more connected with their living and their passing, last lessons well learned.

Is Cancer Stealing Your Time?

Albert Einstein defines time as 'the occurrence of events one after another'. An event is anything that we do. In other words, our life is simply a series of events and activities that occur over the span of our lifetime.

Most events are minor. We plan for them to happen, based upon the choices we make each day.

But some major events we don't plan for, they just happen and usually at the most inconvenient of times. I am talking about a major event like when someone close to you is diagnosed with cancer.

Suddenly our priorities shift and we have a whole new list of activities to add to our already busy schedule and we go in to activity overload!

My father passed away on 3 September 2010. It was his seventy-fifth birthday. He was a time management expert for twenty-three years and was often referred to as 'father time'.

It's fitting, I guess, that he planned his exit from what he referred to as 'spaceship earth' the very same day he arrived, seventy-five years earlier.

The last three months of his life, I was fortunate to have had some deep conversations about the meaning of life, our experiences, and what time really means. I'll never forget the following conversation.

It was early one afternoon, another glorious hot sunny day in Arizona. It must have been 107 degrees outside. We were sitting in his living room just chatting about life and he said this:

Mark, you and I we have been travelling down the highway of life paying no attention to the travellers around us. This highway of life is wide and long, with never ending traffic lanes in either direction. We weave in and out of traffic daily in a hurry to reach our destination. Although our destinations are different from one another, our commonality is that we are travelling on the same path of life.

When one of us gets diagnosed with cancer, it's like a giant crane swings over and picks us up, moving us to the sideline where we are forced to become spectators of life.

In the blink of an eye we get a totally new perspective on life. Suddenly, that destination becomes less important and our priorities change. Instead of fighting for that promotion at work or that next contract, we find ourselves fighting for our life.

It was that day I realised I was taking advantage of time.

It was that day I realised that time is really our most precious commodity. In the end, when we are staring death in the face, it's the events and activities we chose each day that determine our true net worth in life.

I learned a principle that day. I call it the principle of perspective. See, I believe sometimes you and I can be so close to situations, conditions, and opportunities, that we don't really see what's there, we're too close.

In Trapper's case it was terminal cancer. When he was diagnosed it forced him to look at time in a totally different perspective.

For me, it was the experience of watching my father suffer through one of the worst forms of cancer. He never once complained, never wavered from his values, and he continued to teach others until the very day he died.

Let Go & Grow

Losing a parent at any age is difficult. Losing my father when I was eleven years old and my mother when I was twenty-five was devastating. The profound impact that these two life changing events had on me was overwhelming.

For many years previous I had lived the dream. It was the 'goldilocks effect' when everything felt just perfect. A beautiful home, loving supportive parents and a string of siblings who all got on well for the most part. We were seven children in total. Three from my father's first marriage and four from his second marriage after his wife died. I was the youngest and the only girl of the second family. My mother was fifteen years younger than my father and they were so much in love. As a child I felt loved, adored, cherished and somewhat spoilt. A daddy's girl.

The news of my father's terminal oesophageal cancer was broken to me at a very late stage. Perhaps they thought that at eleven I was too young to grasp it. His progression from diagnosis to death was a rapid six months. It was his wish for us children not to visit him in hospital. 1976 had a different set of parenting rules. We waited until his final days when he came home. I remember the feeding tubes in his abdomen and the liquids he would force into them. Most of all I remember his smile and good humour. The rest is a blur.

I guess my coping skills had already started to kick in. The night he eventually died in hospital I had fought with my brother earlier and ran away to find some peace. As I returned to the house hours later I was surprised to see the driveway was full of cars. I thought they were all out looking for me. My feuding brother was the first to greet me and his simple, gentle, sad statement: 'Daddy died', is engraved in my memory for all time. My dear father was only sixty-one years old.

With the formalities of the funeral over, life went back to normal. Except nothing was normal anymore. Everything had changed. Through my teens I threw myself into sport and boyfriends. They gave me a sense of comfort and identity. Academically I didn't care nor did I have any guidance. I was so lost. I think people were afraid to push me or challenge me because I was clearly quite emotionally fragile.

I have recently learned that when one parent dies the other dies too in practical ways. Emotionally, mentally, physically and spiritually their own grief is so overwhelming that they just try to keep functioning as best they can. Guiding four children under the age of sixteen is a huge task for any grieving parent and proved just so for my heartbroken mother.

As siblings we were by now drifting further apart and never really made an effort towards each other. This too was part of our grieving process. Talking about our dad was too painful so we shut down emotionally. Everybody was hurting, everybody was grieving but nobody was getting help or talking about it.

I continued to muddle my way through my late teens with no real direction or guidance. There followed more dead-end jobs and more boyfriends which led to my first child being born when I was twenty-one. My beautiful son gave me a whole new meaning to life and brought me and my mother closer together. Her own grief was still there ten years on but grandchildren seemed to warm her heart once more.

My mother's support during the breakup of my short marriage was unquestionable. She was my rock. Her 'whatever it takes' attitude was remarkable. It's only now when I lie awake thinking about my own children that I realise what I must have put her through during those years. And just as that chapter of our lives came to a close we received her diagnosis. A cancerous tumour at the base of her spine which restricted her mobility and quality of life. Try as she did to maintain her active lifestyle, my fifty-nine-year-old, adorable, funny, glamorous, quirky, beloved mother died a very painful death within six months. No amount of pain relief could make her feel comfortable. Her hair hadn't even grown back when she took her final breath with her whole family standing at her bedside. At least I had got to spend every day with her in hospital during her illness. I never saw such courage and such acceptance. I felt she was somehow glad to be moving on at last. She would be once more reunited with her beloved husband with no more pain and no more suffering.

At twenty-five I was now orphaned. A divorced, trust fund kid with no career, no qualifications and no idea of who I was or what I wanted in life. So I went in search of meaning. Surely there was a purpose to my life. I started to find guidance in books, in influential people, in everyday experiences that gave me a sense of awe and wonder. It was my awakening, albeit through such painful circumstances.

My mistakes I now consider lessons well-learned. At forty-five I still grieve for my parents but embrace their memory every day. I cherish my own children, my brothers and sister and my aunts and uncles. I ask lots of questions about my parents and we share many fond memories.

For the past twenty years I have surrounded myself with positive psychology, health, fitness and wellbeing. I achieved my academic potential by returning to college when I was in my early thirties to study numerous qualifications, the latest being a Master of Science. I am the only member of my family to hold a degree of which I am incredibly proud, as I know what I have had to overcome to get here. My business gurus, including John Butler, gave me a formula and a format for success which I grabbed with both hands and was eager to apply. I worked with head and heart, brain and brawn. Success building on success, confidence and self-worth reaching an all time high.

I still feel a loss when I hear friends talking about their parents. Their joys, their wisdom, their old age. On special occasions I try to mark the day with my own children, remembering their grandparents with some small tribute. I read, I write, I let go and grow. Grieving is a process which no two people experience in the same way. Healing occurs when we face our pain and when we acknowledge what a huge impact losing a loved one has on our lives. I was so numb with pain for so many years that I needed extreme drama in my everyday life just to feel anything. My only suggestion to families in grief is to talk about it. Validate each others' feelings, even through the tears. Get help if you need it, individually or as a family. We owe it to ourselves and our loved ones.

My mantra is 'focus on the compass and not the clock'. As long as I am following my dreams and my life's mission, the time frame is less important. Thankfully my early love of sports has served me well both personally and professionally. My goal is to be the best parent I can possible be to my son and daughter.

Who knows how different my life would be if both of my parents had remained on this earth a bit longer? I am immensely grateful though for the love and support that they showed each other and us children for the short years that I had with them. Their passing is the e-motivation that I embrace as part of my life's journey, giving it meaning and quality. I only hope that they are as proud of me as I am of them and of my own children.

My Gratitude to My Mum

When you are in your twenties, fifty seems like an age it will take forever to reach and quite ancient. Having now reached the age of fifty-six and with the great gift of hindsight, it is now all too obvious to me that fifty is a very young age at which to die. Mum was this age when she lost her battle against cancer. During those fifty years she had lived through so much but sadly was not with us to witness and enjoy many of those things which make a life complete.

Mum was born in 1932 towards the start of the sequence of events in Europe that would impact her early life significantly. At the start of the blitz, when only seven, she was taken from her family in London and evacuated to Wales and then on to Cornwall. It's hard to imagine the absolute trauma of being re-moved from the warmth of a loving family and handed over to total strangers especially those who, in some instances, had little empathy towards the plight of the evacuees. Later in the war, in 1944, she was to be told that her cousin William, who had effect-ively been raised as a brother to her, had been killed in Normandy. Apparently, it was his first drop into enemy territory as a mem-ber of the Parachute Regiment and he was killed soon after land-ing. He was just nineteen.

To have such experiences in the first eleven years of your life would surely break many of us modern day 'softies', but Mum and, I guess, many of her contemporaries, were obviously made from a different mould to us. She had an indefatigable spirit and a way of only looking on the bright side of all she experienced.

It's only now that I fully appreciate the sacrifices Mum made for me and it's now much too late for me to tell her how grateful I am. If only I had said all that I now want to say when I had the opportunity.

Growing up in the fifties and early sixties was a wonderful ex-perience, a time when my main memory is of my sister and I being brought up in a home full of happiness and warmth.

Despite there being one of the coldest winters ever, and us not having much heating in the house, I cannot remember ever being really cold and can only put this down to the one-woman-warmth-creation system that was my mum!

By this time Mum had gone back to work so that we could make ends meet and was working till late most evenings so that her hours did not overlap with Dad's, to ensure someone would be with us at all times. With the increased income in the house Mum and Dad were able to buy us our first television, albeit a rather dodgy second-hand set which could only pick up the BBC and later ITV thanks to the addition of some sort of convertor box which was the size of a desktop computer. What is strange is that I cannot ever remember Mum watching television. There always seemed to be too much for Mum to do to spend time in front of the box. Without fail, irrespective of the time she got home from work, Mum was always the first up in the morning, waiting hand and foot upon the rest of us and ensuring that we got the proper start to our day. How Mum managed to keep going I'm not sure but, at the time, as a young child you just take such things for granted. Again there is so much I should have said to her at the time but, of course, when you're that age it never occurs to you.

Mum's capacity for hard work and her common sense and natural ability to get on with people must have been recognised at the old people's home where she worked as she was promoted to become Deputy Matron. It was at this time when things were getting relatively comfortable that Mum was diagnosed as having rheumatoid arthritis, a crippling, painful disorder causing inflammation of the joints. In particular this affected her hands and feet and must have been immensely debilitating and extremely painful. Her hands were to become gnarled and this made it difficult for her to even hold a cup. Needless to say that such a problem didn't stop Mum from continuing to work or from being the same caring person that she always was. Her last concern was always for herself.

As if the arthritic condition wasn't bad enough, Mum was then diagnosed with Hodgkin's disease, a cancer affecting the lymph nodes. These nodes are all over the body and it is necessary for them to function properly to support the immune system. The treatment for this was primarily doses of chemotherapy which were extremely invasive and each session took Mum a number of days to recover from, the side effects being very unpleasant. It seemed that, despite it all, Mum would keep bouncing back and after recovery from each session she would return to work and to the old routine. She seemed to me to be indestructible and, looking back, I don't think I ever imagined a time when she wouldn't be there. Near her fiftieth birthday Mum was given the news that the problem appeared to be under control. She was especially happy as she didn't think she would reach this age. However, within a matter of months the cancer was back with a vengeance and within seven months of her birthday she had died. The strange thing is that during the time between Mum dying and the funeral, I just felt an emptiness rather than grief, perhaps in shock or subconsciously in denial that it had happened. It seemed to be only after a period of time that grief began, when the reality of knowing that she would never be there again began to dawn.

It may be a cliché but it is so true that the house I grew up in always seemed to be cold and empty after Mum passed away. As someone once eloquently said to describe how they felt upon losing their mother: 'When she left us, the wind went out of our sails.' When she was there, the house with filled with that intangible warmth which made it not just a house but a home. I remember the parties that we had in the house and the way Mum was able to mix with everybody and imbue them with the party spirit (despite her being a teetotaller!) A particular friend of mine would always pop in to see Mum when he passed the house on a Saturday morning even though he knew I would probably be at work. They would sit and chat over a cup of tea and my friend would demolish the contents of the biscuit tin (as I would discover when I returned home!). Mum had this wonderful way of putting people at ease and she was 'a mate to my mates'.

Now I'm just left with the wonderful memories of Mum and so, so many regrets over the things she didn't live to see and the many things I didn't say to her when I had the chance. Thankfully, she did know that my wife and I were planning to get married but never lived to see the wedding. She did at least get to meet my wife's Mum, just the once, and they spent a sunny afternoon 'chilling' in the back garden. It was so good that they did meet. They were similar people in many ways and seemed to get along very well.

The biggest regret though, and rarely a day goes by where I don't think about it, is that she was never to be a granny whilst she was alive. I know that she would have spoilt our children rotten and would have been so proud of the people they are and all that they have achieved. What is also without doubt is that the kids would have loved her too. It's a crazy, foolish notion but I often think of how great it would be if she could only come back for just one day to meet them. Then I tell myself to get real and 'just get on with it' as Mum would have done.

It's said that time is a great healer and in many ways this is true but with time comes life events that bring a joy that I would have loved to share with Mum. Such times inevitably bring with them a regeneration of the grief that never ever really goes away. There is no point in using this grief in a negative way and allowing it to adversely impact the lives of others. That's certainly not what Mum would have wanted and she would only wish that the memory is used in a positive way. So, no matter how difficult it may be at the time, I always remind myself how happy it would make Mum to know that she is always, always in my thoughts.

Poem by Síle Agnew

The Box

False teeth from a dead mouth
sit in a small box on the top shelf
in the creaky wardrobe.

Chewing food and forming words
no longer a task they assist.
The dentures smile
from stationary pink gums.

These enamel coated soldiers
have marched through dinners.
Over the years they have bathed
in Guinness and champagne.
Finally for survival
sucked complan through straws.

In silence they wait for nothing,
yet smile at everything,
from inside the small blue box.

Síle Agnew

Reawakening After Dad's Passing

My father was born in 1930 in New York, USA. At the young age of five my father, his two brothers, sister and my grandparents sold their small grocery store and returned to Ireland to seek a better life. One can only imagine how hard this transition was for all concerned as economic times were very hard, to say the least, both in Ireland and in New York in the early thirties. It is true to say hardships in life mould people and this was true to form for my father.

From an early age, he learned how to work hard and soon traded his youth at first then his whole life for relentless hard and long physical working days on the land. He got married at thirty years of age to my mom and they reared six kids, three boys and three girls. All his life he was a wonderful husband and provider. However, the hard work wore down his emotions day by day making him a generally quiet man who said few words. He loved spending time alone where he could strategise his busy work thoughts for the following days or weeks ahead. Dad loved GAA and his odd trip to his local pub, where he drank his occasional two pints of Guinness as he listened to Traditional music or sometimes even joined in playing a few tunes on his piano accordian. He never retired as farming was his only life and pastime but eventually at the age of seventy-five, he passed to spirit after a two-year illness with cancer.

There were never enough hours in the day for dad. Sometimes it looked like he was punishing himself as the wetter and colder the conditions, the more eager he appeared for himself and his sons to work in it. He loved farming, as it was his vision and purpose in life to provide for his family. I did not understand this vision properly as much as my brothers did, as it appeared to me as plain old simple hard endless work.

After the Leaving Cert., I was pretty much resigned to the fact that farming was not for me and I was given the opportunity to attend university. I graduated at twenty-three and I soon developed similarly high working standards as dad. I got my first job in Agri-sales. As my career progressed, my natural temperament, unbeknownst to myself, had been slightly overshadowed and influenced by my dad's strong-willed and work-focused traits. In a sales environment driven by sales bonus, I embraced it and quickly climbed the various sales positions of the company eventually becoming sales manager.

As a pastime, I loved anything to do with making money. Just like my dad but even more so now, I loved achieving my business goals for the money and praise of the bosses. My life revolved around business and work. I had become a commercial machine and became unaware of my true self and natural emotions making it impossible to sustain intimate relationships. I had no time or respect for any type of relationships to be honest as I had lost touch with all feelings of love, comradeship and general normality.

Looking back, I shudder when I accept and own the traits of the person I became. My desire for financial success, its trappings and its freedom was burning like a forest fire out of control, even up to the day dad passed away on 7 Dec 2005 when I was there by his side talking about various business deals. After the funeral, the months passed and my life started to decay and bit-by-bit fell to pieces. I had lost interest in my career and resigned to take a year out, as there seemed no reason anymore. I could not understand what was going on.

The fulfilment of my career, and life, just left me and everything I once valued seemed meaningless. For three years, I thought the passing of my dad had affected my life adversely. However, on the contrary it was the beginning of my journey backtracking to my youth in search of answers. This backtracking helped me understand my inability to participate in a nourishing symbiotic relationship with my dad, friends and girlfriend at the time.

This self-reflective journey helped me reconnect with my feelings and my own lost soul again. One could say I had a reawakening and began to live daily again with a zest which I had a trait of always doing before my dad's passing. Part of my journey

211

took me to a small village called Devprayag at the top of the Himalayas where the mighty Ganges River forms. It was here I learned that my life was so empty and stagnant and one of the main reasons for this was that I did not have my dad around. For the first time in my life, I realised he was the predominant reason I worked so hard. I used to love telling him of my business achievements and, on many occasions, we disagreed on aspects of my life the way, I was living it. For some reason this push-pull relationship seemed to motivate me even more. For the first time I understood that my dad predominantly worked for the love of his animals and land while I worked for position and financial gain.

We clashed many times on these strong beliefs and I now re-alise that he was living his life with passion and purpose while I was living my life striving for endless financial gain and trophies. He disagreed with my goals being so financially based but I would not listen. At one stage, I naively thought he was jealous of my false, corporate, ego-driven lifestyle compared to his very humble life of working the land. Deep down, looking back in hindsight, I was looking for his approval or any reaction in fact, as compliments were slow coming from a man who suffered so many hardships. He did not believe in a soft up bringing so we were not spoiled with free pocket money. It was there to be earned if we worked for it which we loved doing.

Thankfully today I fully understand the competitive relation-ship I had with my dad and also understand when and where my conscious mind picked up and my subconscious mind stored these beliefs for so many years in my brain. It is fantastic under-standing a man I could never understand growing up. Today I work for passion and purpose in Agri-sales, just like my dad did, whilst farming which helps make my career and achieving my goals so effortless. Thankfully, today I have an incredible zest for life, friendships and future relationships along with achieving work successes, as a mentally and spiritually balanced man. Finding this zest, I owe to my trips to India and its wise teachers whereby I received the wisdom and tools to refocus my life's di-rection and core values and thus reconnect with my soul and strong family values again. They say life is a learning curve. Well I certainly needed my dad to teach me about life's treasured simplicity, life purpose and what hard work was really about. Thank you so much Dad for your wisdom which has made my path is so much clearer today.

Feelings of Mother's Love

I only have short memories of my mother but one thing that remains in my memory is the feeling of love in our home when she was there. As the eldest girl I think I was special to her. There were nine of us altogether aged from ten to one month.

I have vague memories of her complaining of a pain in her stomach or chest. My cousin called that day and I remember him asking would he get the doctor but she said she would be alright.

That night from where I was lying in bed I could see my mother sitting at the fire feeding my little sister. After she put her down to sleep she sat at the fire and I noticed her nodding her head, after a while she didn't raise her head anymore. My father was calling her, when he got no answer he came out of the bedroom took one look at her and grabbed his coat to get help from the neighbours.

During this time I pretended to be asleep, but I knew something terrible had happened. I was aware of an awful thumping in my chest.

When my father and the neighbours came back everything moved fast after that.

I remember a couple of days later when a wooden box was carried out of our house, it didn't register with me that my mother was in it, I was told she was gone to heaven. I didn't understand that as I had no concept of heaven.

Following the death of my mother our family was broken up for good.

Three years later my father died from a massive heart attack. I found it very difficult to talk about my grief for many years. In 1988 I did a course in Basic Counselling Skills and of course I had to tell my story. This was very painful for me and others listening, but I can honestly say it was the start of my healing journey.

In 2006 I did a course with the Bethany Bereavement Support Group and this enabled me to heal further and I found I could help others who were grieving by being compassionate and listening.

My advise to people who are grieving is to talk about it and how they are feeling. It is so important for children to talk and be listened to, it's so vital that they get their feelings out.

When I was a child there was no such thing as counselling so I and my brothers and sisters suffered from suppressed grief. Every bereavement will affect people differently, a lot depends on the relationship one had with the person.

Remember don't suffer in silence and never be afraid to cry – tears are healing.

'A sudden death is like a full stop in the middle of a sentence.'

The Sudden Death of My Father

Year by year you still grieve but it's less painful than it was previously. You will never forget them. They will always be in the back of your mind no matter what.

The truth is that you will never fully get over the sudden death of a loved one, but you can find a way to get through it. Remember this: the people you have lost will always be near you.

Death is a normal life process. We will all experience the death of someone we love. The sudden death of a parent is unmistakably a horrible experience.

There is nothing to compare with the impact and shock of a sudden death. It is a jolt to the system. After a sudden death the period of shock and disbelief is long lasting. Those who have suffered the sudden death of a loved one will experience a long period of numbness and denial.

Everyone deals with the loss of a loved one in different ways. There are so many different feelings that go through your mind due to the loss.

It was Monday evening, I was sitting at the table drawing pictures with my four-year-old son and two-year-old daughter when the phone rang. It was my sister, her words were: 'There is no easy way to tell you this. Dad is dead.' I could feel the life drain from my body. Luckily my husband was home, he took the phone from me and talked to my sister.

My father got a heart attack and died in my mother's arms.

My father was a wonderful, kind, shy and sensitive man. He left school when he was thirteen years old, got a job and worked there for forty-six years. He decided to take early retirement at sixty-two. My parents had four happy years together after working hard and rearing a family. He was sixty-six years old when he died.

He didn't like fuss. He would shake hands, and say: 'Mind yourselves on the road. See you soon', and they were my last words with him.

I arrived at our front door and was greeted by my aunt who caught my arm and told me I had to be brave for my mother and brothers and sisters. The room fell silent as I entered. All I could see was the devastation on my mother s face.

Neighbours, relations and friends stayed with us through the night. They told stories of Dad as a young boy, stories from work, advice he had given to people, things we never knew about him.

I went into superwoman mode making sure people got some rest as it was going to be a long two days. I stayed up all night and the following day. I didn't want that day to end. I was dreading the time when the undertaker would come to take Dad to the church. I will never forget the heartbreak of seeing him leave home for the final time. Dad was a home-bird.

There is an old saying: 'Happy is the corpse that the rain falls on.' If that is true Dad should be very happy as the day of his burial 1 May was cold and wet. We could not linger in the graveyard – it is the way he would have wished it to be.

I returned to Dublin and had to tell my children that Grandad was gone to heaven. It was only then that the realisation of what had happened hit me. I existed in a state of numbness, grieving for myself, his grandchildren that would miss out on so much by not knowing him. I did my grieving in my home and was that brave girl my aunt asked me to be when I went home.

I was afraid to talk about him to mother and my sisters as they were hurting too. I tried to pretend that he was around in the next room. That went on for a while, until one day I went to his grave and told him how much I loved him but I had to let go. This process helped greatly.

That was twenty-five years ago. I still miss him dearly but get great comfort from these verses:

Togetherness
Death is nothing at all
I have only slipped away into the next room
I am I, and you are you
Whatever we were to each other, we still are
Call me by my old familiar name,
Speak to me in the easy way you always used

217

Put no difference into your tone
Wear no forced air of solemnity or sorrow,
Laugh as we always laughed together,
At the little jokes we enjoyed together
Play, smile, think of me
Pray for me
Let my name be the household name as it always was
Let it be spoken without effort
Life means all that it ever meant
It is the same as it ever was
Why should I be out of your mind
Because I am out of your sight?
I am but waiting for you
For an interval
Somewhere very near
Just around the corner
All is well, nothing is passed, nothing is lost,
One brief moment
And all will be as it was before
Only better, infinitely happier and forever
We will be one, together with God.

Henry Scott Holland

God Picks the Best Flowers for His Garden

The problem was I could sense it, feel it, I knew it was going to happen. I told my mum I could feel it. She said nothing but she knew also.

It was just after my eighteenth birthday, the eldest of three children, me a boy, and two younger girls. We had been brought up in a family business my grandfather had started. My dad was the youngest son in a family of five.

His brothers and sister had left home but still worked at home with us in the business because our house was also the office, the garage. They didn't knock to come into our home, they just walked in. Grandad had died before I was born and the business had grown and prospered under his childrens' control. It was a flourishing bus company that had a great reputation of always being on time. The whole business ran like clockwork. Everyone knew what they had to do. There was always tension between the brothers though.

Apparently dad was a tough nut at school and in his youth. He was blind in one eye as a child. Someone had thrown lime into both eyes. I saw him once save a boy's life as he was choking on a lollipop stick and intervene when a man was beating up his wife in the street. He just walked up to him and punched him once and the guy went down, unconscious. His wife then started to berate dad. He just turned round and walked away.

And so it was that 13 October 1974 started the same as any other Sunday. Dad counting the money in the office, me sweeping out the buses. I was playing for the school hockey team later that day. All was well. Then at about 10.30 a.m. dad came into the living room and lay down on the sofa with a pain in his chest. We didn't worry. Mum asked him if he wanted some antacid for indigestion and he didn't seem bothered. After about half an hour I said, 'You had better call an ambulance', and she did. The lady on the phone was very calm. She said an ambulance would be here soon. We rang back after half an hour and still no ambulance.

We rang the local doctor. No reply. Another quarter of an hour and nobody. My Uncle Allan came in and could see it was serious and he said go for the village nurse. I just held dad and he slowly stopped breathing. I don't know why but I sent my sisters out and told them to go for a walk for a while, which they did. I regret this very much now. I ran up to the local Workingman's club for my Uncle Gordon. He was the eldest of the brothers. I saw him in the packed club and said, 'Can you come, Dad's ill.' And everywhere fell silent. They must have heard it in my voice. I ran home to find my Uncle Jim attempting to revive dad. But it was no good. Then the ambulance arrived and left quickly.

I had to tell mum. She was in the other room crying. Uncle Gordon said this is where you have to be a man. I looked up and my sisters had come back. I told them.

The house seemed full of people. Family, friends, everyone. I had to go through his pockets and take off his watch. His ears were blue and I could feel him going cold.

A policeman arrived and took a statement from me.

Billy, the undertaker, took dad away in a coffin and that was that, everyone left. I never cried, I just carried on. I went to bell-ringing and church as normal that night. People said they didn't expect to see me, I couldn't understand why not.

The next day I went to Leek with Uncle Gordon to register his death.

Later that week we had a family meeting, all the brothers and the undertaker.

My uncles started the discussion off. 'You can't get real good oak nowadays,' said Billy. They just stared at him … 'I do have one I was saving up in the loft. I'll get it down. It would be too big for me now anyway. It will be expensive.' Again no comment from anyone. 'I'll do it at the right price though.'

I can't remember much about the intervening ten days except we had several visitors to the door asking for money. We were relatively well off and people must have thought we didn't need it any more. One strange visit was from his friend who asked for his bowls set. I would meet grown men who would burst into tears and several who said they wished it had been them that died because it was so unfair a young man of forty-five dying who was so good and honest. I then started to understand the respect my dad was held in the community. Some people though crossed to the other side of the road to avoid me and my mum. Frankie Baggeley, who sold brake linings to the family business said the most comforting words to mum when he said: 'God always seemed to pick the best flowers for his garden.' That made a difference to her.

It was like a daze or dream, such a lot of flowers, and as we were in the funeral car men stood by the roadside and took off their caps.

I didn't leave dad's grave until everyone else had gone. I don't know why it just didn't seem right leaving him there.

I didn't cry until about twelve years ago when I saw somebody die on TV from a heart attack and it all came back.

I think of him most days and I still feel he will appear at any time. It was a strange feeling to be forty-six. I felt a fraud; I didn't want to 'beat' dad in this way and I always expected to die at the same age as him. I'm now fifty-four and a grandfather and wonder what he would have thought of it all. I miss his guidance when I need it most – making business decisions.

I have been told two things which don't really help. If he didn't smoke he would have survived, and we could have saved him if only we had given him an Asprin.

I don't smoke and I have 75mg of Asprin every day.

I discovered the delay in the ambulance coming was because it came from the town twenty-five miles away. Four years ago I started up a first responder team for our village which is manned by thirty volunteers trained to paramedic standard, at most times complete with a vehicle and flashing lights; ETA (Estimated Time of Arrival) two minutes. Fast enough to administer clot-busting drugs and prevent any more undue pain and suffering.

I don't feel any sadness. What if, is only something I have considered today, having written this document. I am me because of Dad and what happened to him, and subsequently what happened to us as a result. This is in both a physical sense and attitudinally. It's how and what I think and do. As I grow older and look up sharply into a mirror I see him in me. The way he stands in photographs is like me or is it the other way round? The amazing thing is when I look at my grandson I can see the same ways he looks at you as my dad did. What an amazing world we have to savour and enjoy. Perhaps he is still here after all.

So when this happens to you, which it surely will as we are all born of parents, recognise this. Almost everyone will experience it, but it is different for each of us because we each have different views and opinions so there are no rules. However we do have a natural inbuilt ability to cope. Trust it. For some it takes a long while to cope, for others it's much quicker.

However, I do believe it is made easier by the support of others and the following of ceremony or ritual. I believe it is at times like this, that religion is the greatest help. Honed by centuries of experience, they know what's best for most of us.

Our Mum – A Very Special Lady

Our mum was a very special lady though she certainly didn't recognise this but we, her children, know. When she separated from our father, she returned home to Wales where we moved in with another exceptional lady in our lives, our nan. What we lacked for in money, was certainly made up for in love.

Eventually mum met someone else who also had children and so we all moved in together. I shared a bedroom with two step-sisters and a sister, all very cosy with two sets of bunk beds. Life was not easy for mum taking on two children who were not her own and even though this was the case, we were all treated the same, for our mum always had a very big heart.

Some of the special memories I cherish most about mum are the simple things – like the times when I sat beside her at the kitchen table playing with my dolls whilst she baked delicious cakes and I got to enjoy the remainders of the bowl. Or the times when she was getting us ready for school and she always tied ribbons in our hair before sending us on our way with a big hug and a kiss. Then there were the times when we would get sick and she would make us special treats like little individual trifles and she would make soup for us and we were guaranteed to feel much better (a ritual I still follow for myself and for my daughter whenever one of us is sick or feeling low!). Grocery shopping together on Saturday mornings - not a particularly exciting activity but always made more special by knowing that the long walk home with heavy shopping bags would be preceded by a hot vimto and sticky bun in the local café.

Then there was the time when I put a very funny single on the music player (as it was called then) and she and I danced around the living room, singing and laughing at the tops of our voices. And then Sunday lunch … mum would always play her Bobby Goldsboro music whilst preparing lunch for us, and one of my best presents from my husband Mike was Bobby's music which I now play, particularly when I want to remember her.

Whilst mum was not the healthiest of people, as people did not seem to care for themselves in the way they do today, her illness and death still came as a great surprise. I hadn't seen her for a number of months, as I lived in Kent and she lived in Wales. I was on my return from a holiday in Greece and was collected at the airport by my partner. As we waited at the carousel for my suitcases he said I should call home as mum was ill but he didn't say any more than this and he sounded his usual casual self. I telephoned my sister from the airport who told me that mum had been given no more than twenty-four hours to live. You can imagine the shock of that call and receiving that news. My partner and I drove home in virtual silence. I unpacked one suitcase, packed another and we drove through the night, arriving in Wales at around 4.00 a.m. on the Thursday morning.

I went with my sister to the hospital where mum had already been admitted to intensive care and was now on a ventilator. She was swollen and unconscious and lay lifeless in the bed. We were told that she had diverticulitis and septicaemia was now affecting all of her major organs, which were in the process of shutting down. On the Friday she took a turn for the worse and the medical staff suggested taking her into theatre where they would try to cool down her body's extreme temperature. We were warned that she could die in the theatre.

On that unforgettable Friday, my three brothers, my sister and I were there, together with nan and we made all the decisions together as a family. Outside the sun was shining and it was a beautiful day but in the hospital waiting room it just felt cold, dark and timeless.

Mum did come out of theatre and she improved a little in the afternoon but then took another turn for the worse and we were told that it would not be long now. We sat around her bed in a circle; one of my brothers sat on the bed and held mum and we just watched numbly as the monitor slowly ticked downward like a clock until it stopped. It just felt the most surreal thing in the whole world. There was no fuss, no struggle – just the buzzing of the flatline on the monitor and when mum had passed on we all went our separate ways in the hospital to seek some place quiet to try and make sense of what had just happened. Looking back this seems strange as I thought we would somehow have found solace together, but in that moment we each just wanted our own silence and our own space to be with our thoughts.

I can't even remember now if we went back and saw her without all the tubing. I think we did but some things at that time are still a blur whilst others remain crystal clear.

When we left the hospital together in the car and drove out of the gates, the sun was still shining, we could still hear the birds singing and there were children kicking a ball nearby. You could hear their laughter and lightness – only we weren't laughing and the contrast between the feeling in the car and the lightness outside was difficult to comprehend. Speaking for myself, in that moment and place, I simply felt disconnected and wondered how people could still be having fun and going about their business as normal when the day for us had just stopped, and fun was as far away from our thoughts as it could possibly be.

Preparing for mum's funeral was hard and the suit I wore that day was never worn again because of its association. The little chapel in Wales was full and we saw people we hadn't seen in a long while. Whilst we spoke to them all after the funeral and wake, we could not wait for the day to end so we could start to try to come to terms with our loss. Sixty is still young by today's standards and none of us were ready for what had happened.

The hardest part is knowing that as we had all grown up and flown the nest that mum somehow felt she was no longer needed; that everyone had their own lives now. This couldn't have been further from the truth. Our mum, as I am sure others' mums are, was very much needed, always important and though like many perhaps, we might not have said it enough but the bond with your mum is never broken; in life or in death. She had so many grandchildren that loved her and wanted to continue to love her, yet there was not the time. Mum never met my daughter as she came along many years after she had passed on though my daughter carries mum's name as her middle name - Elizabeth. As Grace grows, I will tell her all about mum and also her nan and so she will know how special both were. Unfortunately our nan passed away just a few weeks before Grace was born.

I believe that mum left behind the greatest legacy anyone can; she left to the world five children who benefited greatly from her love, her kindness and compassion, her strong morals, values and teachings. We have all tried to carry these traits forward. She always put others before herself as we have all strived to do. She always cared for those in trouble or suffering, firmly believing in the power of kindness and compassion. She hated seeing people ill-treated or treated unfairly and would go out of her way to support them. She always shared whatever she had, even if it was her last and often it was. Again we all try to follow her strong example and we have all encountered our fair share of challenges in trying to follow mum's example.

I found the process of bereavement difficult but I know it was even more difficult for my sister whose life was very much interwoven with mum's life. I can't pretend to you that the journey is easy and it does take time - often lots; everywhere there are things to remind you of them or tunes on the radio, etc. And so it is a time to be kind to yourself and to be patient and to avoid making hasty decisions. For one day when you wake up, whilst you still remember them, somehow it doesn't hurt quite so much that day as it did the previous day and you start remembering all the good things you did together. The happy feelings and memories start to replace the ones that are sad.

It is then that you start developing your own rituals which help you to remember and recall the special times you shared. I light candles with my daughter on mother's day, mum's birthday and any time I simply want to feel close to her, and we put flowers around the house whilst my sister takes flowers to the cemetery for us.

And I remember the prayer our mum taught us always to say before we climbed into bed each night:

> *Lord, keep us safe this night,*
> *See cures for all our fears.*
> *May angels guard us while we sleep,*
> *Till morning light appears.*
> *Amen.*

And this special prayer will be passed on to our children and their childrens' children. So whilst we still feel the sad loss of our mum, to not have had such a special lady in our lives I know would have been the saddest thing of all.

So on behalf of all your children and grandchildren, mum, I want to thank you from the bottom of all our hearts for being the warm, loving, kind, compassionate and great mum and nan that you were. I know that one day we will all be together again, and until then we ask that God keep you safe for all nights, and protect you with his angels until that time.

To all who read this book and this entry, I pray that you may find comfort in knowing that one day soon you will again enjoy the warmth of the sun on your face and the birdsong, and you will smile again at the laughter of the children as they play and until that time, be patient, kind and loving to yourself knowing that there is no beginning and no end – for life really is but a circle.

With Blessings,
Jane Hamilton (nee Elliott)

Unconditional Love

I 'knew' my mother all my life and forty-five of hers. We didn't have much of a relationship until after my father died when I was twenty-four.

He'd been everything to me prior to his death and there wasn't room for her. Room showed up after his death. Mom was kind of like a nanny – she saw that I was fed, clothed and sheltered. Nothing more.

My mother was hardly a stereotypical mother. For example she didn't tell us, her children, she loved us until we were adults. When I asked her about it when I was in my thirties, her response was: 'Of course I loved you. It went without saying.'

Still we could tell her anything. She <u>never</u> judged us.

Some significant time before she died in 1992, I became aware that there would be a day when I'd no longer be able to visit her so I began to savour even more the time we had together.

In 1988 she was diagnosed with lung cancer. She'd been a two-pack a day cigarette smoker for years. All of her children were ready to mutiny and stop visiting. None of us were smokers and the smoke in the house was overwhelming. She had her surgery and went cold turkey. It was amazing! I, personally, didn't understand why she bothered for the sake of adding 8 minutes a day to her life.

Her illness kept me very conscious that her time with me was likely to be shorter than I would've liked – like, until I died.

A couple of years later cancer showed up in her liver and they treated her with chemotherapy again.

By the spring of 1992, the cancer was spreading. She was having more chemotherapy and I was spending four and a half days a week with her.

For the first time, to my recollection, she expressed worry about me by asking me to call when I got back to home. She'd never asked me to do anything like that before.

Early in 1992, she gave up driving. It was very sad to me.

She'd been fiercely independent and now she was willing not to be. It was a practical thing to do but I found it heart-breaking.

In late August 1992, she was hospitalised. The cancer had metastasized to her brain and high levels of ammonia had accumulated in her system. Once that was reduced she became lucid again.

We brought hospice in. In yet another demonstration of her pragmatic approach to everything, when the hospice aide asked her if she knew what hospice was and why they'd been brought in, Mom said; 'Because I'm going to die.'

My grieving journey began in earnest then - five weeks before her death.

She asked each of her four children to help her take her life. Though we had no problem with her taking her own life, and we'd done the research to know how much medication she would need to accomplish that, we weren't prepared to physically hand her the medication (She had an aide in the house all the time and we couldn't imagine a way for it not to be known that we'd assisted her). Fortunately, for me, she only asked once.

Years before 1992, I'd created a grandmother's book to have some info about hers and my Dad's history. Shortly before she died, I interviewed her and recorded it. I lamented the fact that she'd never worried about me while she always worried about my brothers. 'You never asked me where I was going, who I was going with, when I'd be home. You always asked them.' 'Well,' she said, 'I didn't have to ask you. You always told me.' THAT certainly rewrote my experience of adolescence!

At one point, a week or so before she died, I just sobbed on her chest and told her she couldn't leave me.

She patted my head and told me: 'I've always admired that you could cry.' I was flabbergasted!

She'd chosen to die that year on Rosh Hashonah, Jewish New Year. We all found that quite amusing. We are Jewish in ethnicity. Certainly not by religion.

Part of her adamancy about her death was that she be cremated. About a week before she died, my two younger brothers were in her bedroom with her and all of a sudden there were gales of laughter coming from the room. I'd been in the kitchen and came to hear what was so funny.

'Mom says to incinerate her!' The three of us were laughing so hard at this image that we were crying. (The image conjured up putting her body down an incinerator shoot similar to the one in a closet in the hallway of the floor we lived on when we lived in a high rise apartment building.)

Her response, with hands on her hips as she sat in her wheelchair was: 'It isn't funny!' We laughed harder. She's asked that we all be there when she died and we were. She died on 3 October 1992 at 1.40 p.m., thirteen hours and forty minutes late. It was the only event in her life that any of us had known her to be late for.

When the gentleman from the crematorium came around we picked an urn for her ashes. He wanted to know what we wanted on the piece that would hold a name. We agreed that we only called her 'Eleanor' when we were mad at her. We put 'Mom' on that piece of metal so that when we were bored, or we decided she was, we could turn her upside down and she'd be 'Wow'.

A week after she died, I was facilitating a section of a workshop on raising super kids. It was a video workshop and, as I watched, it struck me that she'd loved us unconditionally. I'd never seen that before. I realised at the same time that she had us all with her when she died; not for her benefit, but for ours.

Lessons Learned:
1. Love your children and let them know it
2. Never stop laughing while the dying is going on. We laughed with each other, at her and with her for the six months before she died. It was, and remains an invaluable gift.
3. Grieve as <u>you</u> need to, not as others say is right or appropriate. Personally, I purchase a Mother's Day card for her every year. I purchase a birthday card from me to her and a card from her to me every year. Occasionally, I write a letter to her and have written at least one from her to me. When things get tough, open your heart.

4. If the dying process takes a while, be OK with yourself if you begin to resent the person who is ill. It's not personal, and you're not 'bad'. It's hard on everyone and caregivers are often given short shrift.
5. It's OK to feel relief when death does occur. It makes you no less worthy.
6. Remember that often, most of us say 'stupid' things in uncomfortable situations. Be forgiving of the people who do that after your loss (and don't hang around them much).
7. Learn empathy for others who are experiencing losing loved ones or have lost them without warning. My Dad died of an aneurysm. Mom took a while. For me, I wasn't prepared either way.
8. You cannot ever be completely prepared. One of the things I knew I'd miss was being able to do anything for her after she died. So I did everything I could for her while she was alive. Being able to help in the smallest of ways was strengthening for me. I had control over those errands or whatever and no control over the fact that she was going to die.
9. Find good books to read on grieving. Two I've come to know and recommend are *The Grief Recovery Handbook* by John James and Russell Friedman and *How to Survive the Loss of a Love* by Harold H. Bloomfield, MD *et al*.

My grieving journey continues. There are times I cry for missing her or cry just because. Instead of squelching it because I'm embarrassed I remember that she admired that I could cry and so I honour her when I do. The birthday cards from her to me for this year are on my desk waiting to be signed. Her 2011 Mother's Day card is on top of her urn.

Inspired by My Mum

Thirty years ago when I was twenty, my Mum passed away. She was only forty six years old. Her, my dad and my younger brother, who was twelve, were away on a holiday in Yugoslavia. They had just returned from a trip to Venice and had sat down to dinner. My Mum suffered a massive heart attack, slumped on to the table and died. My sister and I were at home so did not know what had happened. That night the dog went berserk and wouldn't stop barking! There was a peculiar call from my Granny. The family were waiting for my Dad to get home to tell us. It was four days before my Dad and brother could get back home. My sister and I expected them all home on Sunday. The doorbell rang early on Saturday morning and I jumped out of bed to answer it with my sister following behind.

When I opened the door my dad was there with all his brothers and sisters – shock washed through me. I cried privately for a year. At the end of that year I was engaged and married a year later. I was delighted my Mum had met my husband and I knew I had her absolute approval. The tears began to dry up at that point.

I am now fifty years old and have lived a marvellous life full of great love, experiences and learning. Now, all these years later, I know the tears were all about me. I was not ready for this experience – the pain was intolerable and I was struggling to deal with this new reality.

Change is challenging and missing your Mum is a struggle. Knowing that Mum would no longer be there when I needed her, demanded that I 'get on with it'. However, I have discovered that for me there are no goodbyes!

My Mum has taken great care of me during the last thirty years. Without her, and all my other friends and relatives who left me, I don't think I'd be where I am today. They have inspired me, uplifted me and encouraged me. I hear their guidance as I make choices about my life. Their guidance has inspired my family life, my career and many decisions I have made. I see them alive; alive in a different place. While I can't see them, I know they are watching over me at all times. I can always turn to them and ask for guidance. I have found this comforting and soothing.

While readjusting to the change, I came to experience this comfort and allowed my Mum to continue minding me.

I believe in a life after death.
A life after death I don't understand now!
But I will understand when I move into that stage of my life.
However it is great to be fully alive and enjoying this place.
Life holds no fear.
Death holds no fear.
Life is to be lived without fear.
Death is to be lived without fear.

I feel lucky and blessed to be minded by those who have moved to another place in the last thirty years. I now know the pain I felt was my pain because the person has died and because I was not in the emotional place where I could deal with it.

CHAPTER SIX

Adapting to the Change

Life is eternal, and love is immortal, and death is only a horizon;
and a horizon is nothing save the limit of our sight.
Rossiter Worthington Raymond

Change and transformation are terms which I am very familiar with through the work of our consulting business. Our work involves facilitating individuals, teams and businesses as they change and transform their thinking, behaviours and approach to their business, with the aim of increasing performance, productivity and results.

We challenge individuals to break through their old thinking and adapt new methodologies and practices. We encourage people to leave their comfort zones and change and transform and be different.

So you might think that I as a 'change agent' would be familiar and ready to adapt to any change, even one of major significance in my life on the death of my partner and husband. But let me tell you, nothing – no knowledge, theory or past experience – prepares you for the great loss of your loved one. Everyone who has been through this journey knows what I am talking about. You know the pain, the sorrow, the loss, the sadness and the sheer brokenness of life that follows.

Nature shows us that caterpillars are transformed into the beautiful butterflies we love to see flying around on a summer's day. There is no going back for the humble caterpillar. Similarly there is no going back for the bereaved; no possibility of bringing back our dearly beloved.

Change is about becoming different. We know in business the best time to initiate change is when the company is prosperous and the change is not a necessity. In many ways the opposite principle applies to learning to live without the presence of your loved one. There appears to be no best time to say goodbye and change. There is only now.

There is a four phase *Lifecycle* model that applies to work and life, which I would like to share because of its value to the grieving process.

The Four Lifecycle Phases

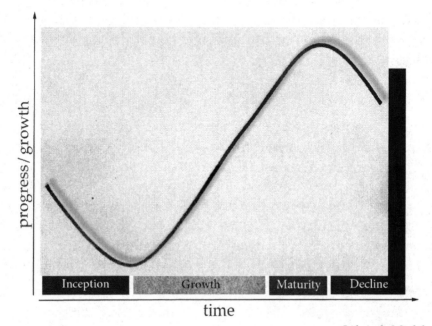

Lifecycle Model

Phase One: is the birth and early childhood phase. This is very much a dependent phase where the child relies on their parents for everything.

Phase Two: is the youth and vigorous stage, where children integrate and become part of society through learning and education.

Phase Three: is the earning stage, where career and business objectives are met and intellectual and emotional maturity resound.

Phase Four: is viewed as the contribution phase where one considers making a difference and 'leaving a legacy' as they move into the autumn years of life.

How shocking for anyone whose progress and time have been cut short by the early departure of a loved one. There is no knowing what length that journey is for each person; no telling which stage of the chart each individual will reach. No label at birth states our life expectancy. Would it help us to know? I doubt it. It may just bring additional stress and grief to our lives.

The secret is captured in the saying: 'Live every minute of every day like it's your last, because you never know what tomorrow will bring.'

The Change Model

In business I have always loved the simple Kurt Lewin model on change. Now I can connect with the model in my grieving process. From a business perspective, change and transformation management is more concerned with how organisations adapt to new trends, how they react to competitors, and how they meet ever-changing customer needs. How do you change a square block of ice (your present condition) into the new form of a triangle (your desired state)? This is the classic question which provides a preface to Kurt Lewin's work on change.

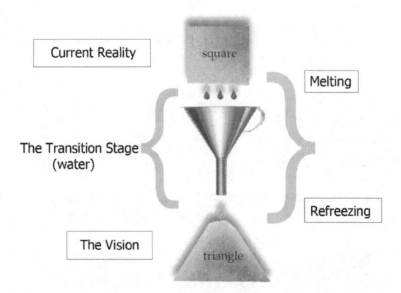

Change Model – Kurt Lewin

The Change Process

In business, you can use two methods to accomplish the change process. The first method is the *hammer approach,* often used in times of crisis or as a last resort. In this approach, you use the hammer to smash the ice-cube and force the pieces into the form of a triangle. The advantage of the *hammer approach* is that it can be accomplished very quickly. However, more often than not, the result is not a smooth fit with the desired new state.

This tends to lead to endless resistance, cynicism, and only token commitment in the workplace. With this approach, you tend to move bodies, not minds. A complete transformation requires physical commitment (the hands to do the work), mental awareness (the head to think about it) and cultural or emotional responsibility (the heart to value it).

You have a second option. Change the square ice-cube into a triangle by unfreezing the ice-cube and gradually guiding the liquid to the point where it can be refrozen into the form of a triangle. This *unfreezing, changing* and *refreezing* method usually takes longer. Having said that the result is the desired new structure, shaped according to a plan and with the all-important commitment from everyone. You are more likely to win hands, heads and hearts with this process.

The ice-cube model demonstrates the change process. How to successfully implement such a change is one of the biggest challenges for all managers and organisations today.

In grieving the process is similar. Whether you have been hit with a *hammer,* by sudden death, or *melted* into it, by a long illness, death is still death. It is final and it challenges us to reshape our lives.

The melting process of adjusting every aspect of your life without your deceased loved one is a long and arduous journey. It takes time to work through all the memories and emotions to eventually arrive at a place where you can feel comfortable again in your new state.

The Kurt Lewin model gives us an appreciation for creating the new shape. In our family we referred to the change process by saying: 'Our family unit was a four-legged chair – now the new shape is a three-legged stool.' It is still functional but misses all the old support of the chair.

> *To live in hearts we leave behind is not to die.*
> Thomas Campbell

CHAPTER SEVEN

The SARAH Process

There have been many fine books written on the subject of bereavement. A true pioneer of the subject was Dr Elisabeth Kübler-Ross who wrote a number of books on the subject including *On Life After Death*. In this book she presented a five-stage approach to grief.

In our consulting business, we developed a five phase approach in our client work called *the SARAH process*, to help people understand the change process. It follows a process of **S**hock, **A**nger, **R**ejection, **A**cceptance and **H**ealing. We use the acronym SARAH to outline the process and at this point I would like to apologise to anyone named Sarah for your name being used in this context.

When our clients are struck by a crisis or have change forced upon them we recommend that they follow *the SARAH process*. When the realisation finally hits them, usually in the form of a major customer leaving or a significant shift in their marketplace, the degree to which they implement this process will determine whether they will survive or not. What we have found is that if they manage their journey successfully, then they will be better able to cope with the long-term effects of change.

Ironically, the same system applies to the grieving process. I caution that this is an ongoing journey and not something that we can say: 'Yes, I did the five steps and should be fixed now.' That is not how grieving effects us. Though we continue on our journey, our hearts will never forget that we have loved and lost. It is an ongoing process, and a long-term journey of healing.

The SARAH Process: Managing a Change Crisis

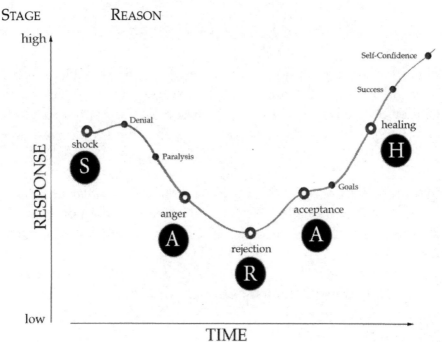

SARAH Model

Shock   You are jolted by the horrendous shock of the death of your loved one. The sheer trauma of not seeing them alive ever again can be overwhelming.

Example: You get the call to come home; you are there at the bedside; you are told the harrowing news. He is dead; she is dead. The first emotional response can be immobilisation and shock, frozen to the spot where you stand or sit. The thought: 'It couldn't happen to us, this cannot be true', may strike you.

Anger   Anger and hurt rise to the surface as you ask *why?* Then blaming and confusion can occur as the reality of the situation becomes too much to bear.

Example: Why? Why? Why? But we were so happy; we loved each other; there was so much more we wanted to

240

do together! Then there may be the Blame! Blame! Blame! 'Why did the medical team not do more? Why did God let this happen?' Fear of loss, letting-go, and all manner of emotions can come to the fore under such circumstances.

Rejection   Many individuals reject or resist this major trauma through the usage of cliches or platitudes such as: 'Isn't he better off now', 'Her suffering is over' and 'Sure wasn't he a great age'.

Example: For some people it is a denial of reality. Some people busy themselves in order to detract from the truth. They deny the reality of this awful situation. Depression levels can increase … production levels decrease … stress increases … focus and clarity decreases.

Acceptance   Gradually, you begin to accept that the loss of your loved one will have serious repercussions for your life.

Example: There will have to be major changes in your life. The times and lives shared are no longer and accepting this can be very challenging. Recognising that your heart is like a precious Waterford crystal vase that has been shattered into pieces – broken, dislocated and permanent ly wounded - is not easy. Yet as winter turns to spring; per haps death will bring a new life and a new, different 'norm'.

Healing   People have an amazing capacity to regenerate and recover from traumatic events. You will start to heal and accept the inevitable. Healing and hope go hand in hand. More importantly, a new sense of purpose emerges for almost everyone in the grieving process.

Example: As you come to terms with the pain of loss, so too a healing process begins to restore purpose, clarity and energy to your life.

The SARAH Process can bring understanding to the grieving journey. It may not be the best system in the world, but my contention is that any system is better than no system. I personally find it helpful in giving me an appreciation of where I am on the journey. And I realise that it is a very dynamic process, one on which you journey back and forth. For example, I thought I was doing quite well on letting John go until recently, when I heard a song on the radio. This song affected something within me and brought me right back along the journey to take that one memory through *the SARAH process*. At least I knew what was happening and I had a process to help me journey with my emotions and memories.

The grieving process can be traumatic for a long time in the aftermath of the initial shock. You can lessen that trauma by understanding that change is a journey that takes time and may be hindered by many obstacles before you once again achieve happiness, reassurance and confidence.

The SARAH process is one way to 'travel' through a distressing period of change or a crisis. The objective is to understand where you are in the process. Many people risk getting stuck at any one stage of the process rather than addressing and processing the emotional, even natural, responses. If only they knew that anger and negative resistance is often the storm before the calm, then perhaps they would wait out the storm. Only then can they move towards acceptance and healing.

> *Learn to get in touch with the silence within yourself, and know that everything in life has a purpose. There are no mistakes, no coincidences, all events are blessings given to us to learn from.*
> Elisabeth Kübler-Ross

CHAPTER EIGHT

Creating New Beginnings

Values shape your character, energise your life and fast-forward your decision-making capability.

People who have been bereaved sometimes ask: 'What's it all about? Why and how can I continue?' Indeed the same thought struck me more than once on my grieving journey. What encourages me along the way is my belief that I have core values and a mission or purpose to fulfill; and when that work is done – I too will be complete.

I recall saying to our daughters as we talked in our kitchen: 'John fulfilled his purpose in life, so his time to depart was now.' The reply I got from one of our daughters was: 'Well if life is about fulfilling your purpose – I'm going to get such a big purpose that I'll never die.'

In my opinion, values are at the very heart of what makes you who you are. They are your guiding compass. They are your central decision-making guide. For example, if you value honesty, you are unlikely to steal from your neighbour. Your values energise your talents and help align them with your purpose and destiny. Values shape your character. Your values are the fuel in the fire of your personal purpose and strategy. Your core values determine who you are and how you do what you do. Your values are at the very epicentre of your 'being'.

A personal value can be described as 'what is important and significant to you as a human being.' Values are your central belief system and crystallise your perception of 'what is right' for you. Personal values are procedures, more like habits. They do not depend on fear to be put into practice. Personal freedom and choice are the essential bedrocks of values. You can, of course, learn to implement a new value simply by practising it in every possible situation.

Charles Reade wrote: 'Sow an act, and you reap a habit. Sow a habit and you reap a character. Sow a character and you reap a destiny.'

You may well ask, what role do values play in guiding you through the grieving process? Values provide a framework for decision-making in your life. They also provide a basis for action and help you to live with the results of your actions. Values are your unifying principles and core beliefs and provide the anchor point of your personal life.

Thomas Jefferson said: 'In matters of principle, stand like a rock.' When you bring clarity to who you are on the inside, only then can you determine a clear focus on the outside for your future direction. You may have discovered that many well-meaning people try to help by giving advice, or trying to advise you on what to do and how to do it, at times of grief. This is when your core values are really important and help you stand for what you believe to be right to do and fend off the many well-intentioned but ill-advised pieces of advice or opinions. The one thing you know for certain is that life as you knew it has changed and will never be the same again.

So the question is: 'What is important in your life from here on?' Resetting your core values will help frame that new norm. Core values allow you to create your 'new norm' and your new life shape. All change in your personal or professional development begins by clarifying and ordering your true values and then committing yourself to live by them. James Allen once said: 'All that there is to making a successful, happy and beautiful life is the knowledge and application of simple root principles.' As Joan Baez put it: 'You don't get to choose how you are going to die. Or when. You can decide how you're going to live. Now.'

In the world of business the core values of an organisation can determine its culture and way of doing business. Too often, however, rules, laws and procedures set boundary lines such as: 'If you break this rule you will be penalised', or 'You will be in trouble if ... ' Negative cultures breed fear and inhibitions and take endless time to police. Positive cultures empower people to be more creative and productive. 'All that is necessary for the triumph of evil is that good men do nothing' are the immortal words of Edmund Burke in the 18th century.

Hippocrates – the father of medicine – set the first medical values over two thousand years ago when he advised doctors to *'Primum non nocere'* (First, do no harm). Mahatma Gandhi crystallises the importance of values as follows: 'It's the action, not the fruit of the action that's important. You have to do the right thing. It may not be in your power, it may not be in your time, that there'll be any fruit. But that does not mean you stop doing the right thing. You may never know what results from your action. But if you do nothing, there will be no result.'

The formation of your 'new' core values is an important part in rebuilding your life after the death of your loved one. The real foundation of a happy, healthy, self-confident lifestyle is living a life consistent with your core values. When you have total clarity and inner acceptance in this area, you accept yourself unconditionally as a valuable and worthwhile person and this is what fuels your life with renewed purpose.

So, what are your personal and family values now? You were certain of them for so long – but now this change raises the question. All the great values are simple and can often be expressed in a single word or short phrase. What is your attitude to your family? Your health? Your work, career, business? Your friends? Your God?

How do you write a set of values?
The mechanics of engaging in a values exercise is relatively simple. Just brainstorm keywords and phrases that constitute your personal values and what is important to you.

Good questions to help trigger your thoughts are:
- What do you do that gives you the most pride?
- What is really satisfying about what you do?
- What do you stand for / What do you not stand for?
- What do you hold dear?
- What do you really value?

The next part of the exercise is to craft the keywords and phrases into value statements.

Core Values Statements are:
- To live my life with honesty and integrity.
- To be excellent in all my family relationships.
- To be financially independent.
- To enjoy my career to its fullest.

A personal value statement is often a simple, straightforward encapsulation of the obvious. The order is important, however. You need to consider alternatives and grade them in order of importance. Ranking them in order of importance is an imperative. Why? If you do not, you can trade one off against the other.

In the example above, nothing supersedes 'honesty and integrity'. Here, integrity is first and foremost, then family, then money, then career. If this person were to throw away three, the one kept would be integrity. This is the test. Do you feel good about your values? Are you happy to talk publicly about your value positions and views?

Many people struggle with conflicting values. The act of committing your values to paper and reviewing them on a regular basis brings clarity and helps to decipher what is important to you. They help you to leapfrog procrastination, fear of failure and negativity blocks. They help with communications, motivation and learning. They may also bring contentment, thus allowing you to focus on higher order work and your purpose in life. Clarifying and ordering your values is, ultimately, a statement of how you will live your life from this moment in time onwards.

Allow me to share an example with you about our family. John wrote the book, *Crossing the Rubicon*, which included a chapter and guidance on setting your values. So it should come as no surprise to learn that we both had our personal values, our combined relationship values and our family values; identifying what was important to us in the different areas of our lives. We also had our business values. Of course there was overlap as we were both the common denominator in all areas.

So when John died, our core values were broken into smithereens. What had been a four-legged chair, now became a three-legged stool. Our two daughters and I went away for a break and took some time over dinner to chat about what is important to us now as a threesome in our newly-shaped family. And in so doing we came up with our new set of values on what is important to us as a family. We found the exercise encouraging, refreshing and helpful in laying the foundation for the new 'norm' which we are addressing in our family.

I recommend you take time to talk with your loved ones about what is important to you and to them. Then you can put some shape on your new lives together without the presence of your dearly beloved departed member. Take time to develop a new set of core values of what is important to you and your life.

The most beautiful people we have known are those who have known defeat, known suffering, known struggle, known loss, and have found their way out of the depths. These persons have an appreciation, sensitivity, and an understanding of life that fills them with compassion, gentleness, and a deep loving concern. Beautiful people do not just happen.
Elisabeth Kübler-Ross

CHAPTER NINE

Crystallising Your Purpose

What is your life all about? What is your purpose? What is your calling? How are you going about doing what you have to do?

Your new life demands a response to each of the questions posed above. I believe that your mission statement will help you, in time, to regain clarity and focus in your life. Your mission statement should be a broadly-based, enduring statement of purpose that distinguishes you from your peers or 'similar individuals'. It explains the reason for your existence. It crystallises and articulates your values, dreams and behaviours. It is about how you aspire to do things. It is your guiding light.

Your mission statement should define your purpose in life. Your mission becomes a way of life for you, almost like a vocation. It should combine who you are with what you do, where you are coming from with where you are going. When you are 'working on purpose' you are happy and 'in the zone'. People with purpose rarely 'go to work'. Work instead becomes full of meaning and direction. In a nutshell, it's what you are about.

Crafting your mission statement is a relatively simple task if you follow a system. Capturing your thoughts in the form of words is the big challenge. It's like writing your legacy in advance. Your mission, of course, should evolve from your values statement.

Herbert Casson, the philosopher, once wrote: 'To have a purpose that is worthwhile and that is steadily being accomplished, that is one of the secrets of a life that is worth living.' Your mission statement encapsulates the answers to the questions posed above. It captures the driving forces of your internal engine in one simple sentence. Crafting your mission statement from a mixed bag of descriptive words and phrases and distilling these words into one cogent sentence is often a soul-searching, but rewarding exercise. This exercise is at the core of your healing process.

Mission Statement examples:

- My ultimate mission in the world is to make a significant difference in the lives of the less fortunate.
- My mission is to achieve my full potential as a professional and be fully alive in doing this.

Writing a mission statement brings clarity, focus and power to your current reality and future direction. Lack of clarity and diffused effort can be the causes of lost opportunity and stress. When you write down your enduring statement of purpose, you are forced to meet yourself on the page. This may take longer than you expected. Do not be put off if you still aren't satisfied after several attempts. Eventually, through the various drafts and edits, your sixth sense will know which words to choose.

Over time, your mission helps you to develop a quiet confidence and an immeasurable strength to handle the challenges that life throws at you. Type it up, put it in your wallet with a photo of your loved ones and read it at odd moments in time. In so doing, you will confirm to yourself that you are living on purpose.

Beware of the cynic within you that scoffs at such an exercise. Be aware that the laughter of others is their defence mechanism, as to their rationale for not completing such an exercise. In other words, be clear as to the importance of writing a mission or purpose statement. Then take courage and 'just do it' as the Nike slogan says.

One of the big regrets for many older people is that they do not bring clarity and focus to their purpose in life much earlier as crystallised in the immortal words of Oliver Wendell Holmes: 'Most people die with their music still in them.' I recommend that you define and clarify your purpose in life and live it fully with focus, passion and love.

THE LEGACY OF STEVE JOBS

Steve Jobs, the founder and creative genius of Apple Inc., died on 5 October 2011. In 2005, shortly after he was diagnosed with cancer, he presented a wonderful speech in his address at Stanford University (USA). I quote him directly as I consider his inspiration to be part of his great legacy to the world.

'The only way to do great work is to love what you do. If you haven't found it yet, keep looking. Don't settle. As with all matters of the heart, you'll know when you find it.'

When I was seventeen, I read a quote that went something like: 'If you live each day as if it was your last, someday you'll most certainly be right.' It made an impression on me, and since then, for the past thirty three years, **I have looked in the mirror every morning and asked myself: 'If today were the last day of my life, would I want to do what I am about to do today?' And whenever the answer has been 'No' for too many days in a row, I know I need to change something.**

Death is the destination we all share, no one has ever escaped it. And that is as it should be because death is very likely the single best invention of life.

Your time is limited, so don't waste it living someone else's life. Don't be trapped by dogma — which is living with the results of other people's thinking. Don't let the noise of others' opinions drown out your own inner voice. And most important, have the courage to follow your heart and intuition. They somehow already know what you truly want to become. Everything else is secondary. **Remembering that I'll be dead soon is the most important tool I've ever encountered to help me make the big choices in life.** Because almost everything — all external expectations, all pride, all fear of embarrassment or failure — these things just fall away in the face of death, leaving only what is truly important. **Remembering that you are going to die is the best way I know to avoid the trap of thinking you have something to lose. You are already naked. There is no reason not to follow your heart.**

No one wants to die. Even people who wanna go to heaven don't wanna die to get there.'

I would like to express a final word of appreciation to our wonderful contributors who dug deep into their hearts to recall their stories, to heal and support themselves and others on the grieving journey of life.

Finally thank you, the reader. We wish you a good life full of hope and love and a sense of peace, from living your purpose.

> *The only way to do great work is to love what you do.*
> *If you haven't found it yet, keep looking. Don't settle.*
> *As with all matters of the heart,*
> *you'll know when you find it.*

CHAPTER TEN

Reflections

The following passages and reflections have been donated by
readers who have found solace through the verses.

Be Not Afraid

You shall cross the barren desert, but you shall not die of thirst.
You shall wander far in safety though you do not know the way.
You shall speak your words in foreign lands and all will understand.
You shall see the face of God and live.

Be not afraid.
I go before you always.
Come follow me, and
I will give you rest.

If you pass through raging waters in the sea, you shall not drown.
If you walk amid the burning flames, you shall not be harmed.
If you stand before the pow'r of hell and death is at your side,
know that I am with you through it all.

Be not afraid.
I go before you always.
Come follow me, and
I will give you rest.

Blessed are your poor, for the kingdom shall be theirs.
Blest are you that weep and mourn, for one day you shall laugh.
And if wicked men insult and hate you all because of me,
blessed, blessed are you.

I Am Not Gone

I am not gone
      While you cry with me
I am not gone
      While you smile with me
I am not gone
      While you remember with me

I will come
      When you call my name
I will come
      When I feel your pain
I will come
      On your final day

It could never be
      That we
            Would never be

We shall always
      Be together
            Forever

I am not gone
                        Michael Ashby

23rd Psalm

The Lord is my Shepherd; I shall not want.
He maketh me to lie down in green pastures:
He leadeth me beside the still waters.
He restoreth my soul.

My First Christmas in Heaven

I see the countless Christmas trees around the world below
With tiny lights, like heaven's stars, reflecting on the snow.
The sight is so spectacular, please wipe away the tear
For I am spending Christmas with Jesus Christ this year.

I hear the many Christmas songs that people hold so dear
But the sounds of music can't compare with the Christmas choir up here.
I have no words to tell you, the joy their voices bring,
For it is beyond description, to hear the angels sing.

I know how much you miss me, I see the pain inside your heart
But I am not so far away, we really aren't apart.
So be happy for me, dear ones, you know I hold you dear.
And be glad I'm spending Christmas with Jesus Christ this year.

I sent you each a special gift, from my heavenly home above.
I sent you each a memory of my undying love.
After all, love is a gift more precious than pure gold
It was always most important in the stories Jesus told.

Please love and keep each other, as my Father said to do
For I can't count the blessing or love he has for each of you.
So have a Merry Christmas and wipe away that tear
Remember, I am spending Christmas with Jesus Christ this year.
Author Unknown

He is Gone

You can shed tears that he is gone,
Or you can smile because he lived.

You can close your eyes and pray that he will come back,
Or you can open your eyes and see all that he has left.

Your heart can be empty because you can't see him
Or you can be full of the love that you shared.

You can turn your back on tomorrow and live yesterday,
Or you can be happy for tomorrow because of yesterday.

You can remember him and only that he is gone
Or you can cherish his memory and let it live on,

You can cry and close your mind,
be empty and turn your back,
Or you can do what he would want:
smile, open your eye, love and go on.
David Harkins

Peace At Last

May the Lord support us all the day long
Till the shades lengthen and the evening comes,
And the busy world is hushed,
And the fever of life is over,
And our work is done.
Then in his mercy,
may he give us a safe lodging,
A holy rest and peace at the end.
Amen.
Blessed John Henry Newman

Miss me, but let me go

When I come to the end of the road,
and the sun has set for me,
I want no rites in a gloom-filled room.
Why cry for a soul set free?

Miss me a little – but not too long,
and not with your head bowed low.
Remember the love that was once shared.
Miss me, but let me go.

For this is a journey we all must take,
and each must go alone.
It's all a part of the master's plan,
a step on the road to home.

When you are lonely and sick of heart,
go to the friends we know.
Bear your sorrow in good deeds.
Miss me, but let me go.
Author Unknown

The Lord's Prayer

Our Father who art in heaven,
hallowed be thy name.
Thy kingdom come,
thy will be done,
on earth as it is in heaven.
Give us this day our daily bread;
and forgive us our trespasses,
as we forgive those who trespass against us;
and lead us not into temptation,
but deliver us from evil.
For thine is the kingdom, the power
and the glory, forever. Amen

A Prayer of St Francis

Lord, make me an instrument of Thy peace;
where there is hatred, let me sow love;
where there is injury, pardon;
where there is doubt, faith;
where there is despair, hope;
where there is darkness, light;
and where there is sadness, joy.

O Divine Master, grant that I may not so much seek
to be consoled as to console;
to be understood as to understand;
to be loved, as to love.
For it is in giving that we receive;
it is in pardoning that we are pardoned;
and it is in dying that we are born to Eternal Life.
Amen.

Thoughts to Live By

Keep Your Thoughts Positive,
Thoughts Become Your Words.
Keep Your Words Positive,
Words Become Your Behaviours.
Keep Your Behaviours Positive,
Behaviours Become Your Habits.
Keep Your Habits Positive,
Habits Become Your Values.
Keep Your Values Positive,
Values Become Your Destiny.
Mahatma Gandhi

Leaving a Dear One

The family is not destroyed
but transformed.
A part of it enters the invisible.

We believe that dying leads to absence,
when it really is a hidden presence.
We believe it creates infinite distance,
when it does away with all distance.
It returns to the Spirit,
what was for a time found in the flesh.

Every time someone leaves home and passes away,
those left behind gain a link in heaven.

Heaven is no longer home to angels,
Unknown saints and a mysterious God,
but it becomes familiar.
It is the family house,
the house up above, so to speak,

From up there to down here,
Memory, helping hands, calls carry on.
F. Sertillanges

Grief

Grief cannot be shared, for it is mine alone.
Grief is a dying within me,
a great emptiness,
a frightening void.
It is loneliness, a sickening sorrow at night,
on awakening a terrible dread.
Another's words do not help.
A reasoned argument explains little
for having tried too much.
Silence is the best response to another's grief.
Not the silence that is a pause in speech,
awkward and unwanted,
but one that unites heart to heart.
Love, speaking in silence, is the way into
the void of another's grief.
The best of all loves comes silently,
and slowly too, to soften the pain of grief,
and begins to dispel the sadness.
It is the love of God, warm and true,
which will touch the grieving heart and heal it.
He looks at the grieving person and has pity,
for grief is a great pain.
He came among us to learn about grief,
and much else too, this Man of Sorrows.
He knows. He understands.
Grief will yield to peace – in time.
Cardinal Basil Hume, OSB

Take Time

Take time to think;
It is the source of all power.

Take time to read;
It is the foundation of all wisdom.

Take time to play;
It is the source of perpetual youth.

Take time to be quiet;
It is the opportunity to seek God.

Take time to be aware;
It is the opportunity to help others.

Take time to love and be loved;
It is God's greatest gift.

Take time to laugh;
It is the music of the soul.

Take time to be friendly;
It is the road to happiness.

Take time to dream;
It is what the future is made of.

Take time to pray;
It is the greatest power on earth.

Take time to give;
It is too short a day to be selfish.

Take time to work;
It is the price of success.
Author Unknown

Will you meet me at the Fountain?

Will you meet me at the Fountain
When I reach the glory land?
Will you meet me at the Fountain
Shall I clasp your friendly hand?
Other friends will give me welcome,
Other loving voices cheer,
There'll be music at the Fountain,
Will you meet me there?

Will you meet me at the Fountain?
I shall long to have you near
When I meet my loving Saviour,
When His welcome words I hear.
He will meet me at the Fountain,
His embraces I shall share.
There'll be glory at the Fountain,
Will you, will you meet me there?
Author Unknown

The Dash

There was a man who stood to speak,
At the funeral of a friend.
He referred to the dates on her tombstone,
From the beginning to the end.

He noted that first came her date of her birth,
And spoke the following date with tears.
But he said what mattered most of all,
Was the dash between those years.

For that dash stands for all the time,
That she spent alive on earth.
And now only those who loved her,
Know what that little line is worth.

For it matters not how much we own;
The cars, the house, the cash.
What matters is how we live and love,
And how we spend our dash.

So think about this long and hard.
Are there things you'd like to change?
For you never know how much time is left,
That can still be rearranged.

If we could just slow down enough,
To consider what's true and real,
And always try to understand,
The way other people feel.

We'd be less quick to anger,
And show appreciation more,
And love the people in our lives,
Like we've never loved before.

If we treat each other with respect,
And more often wear a smile,
Remembering that this special dash,
Might only last a little while.

So when your eulogy is being read,
With your life's actions to rehash,
Would you be proud of the things they say,
About how you spent your dash?
Linda Ellis

Commitment

Until you are committed there is hesitancy,
the chance to draw back,
always ineffectiveness.

Concerning all acts of initiative,
there is one elementary truth,
the ignorance of which kills countless ideas
and splendid plans:
the moment you definitely commit yourself,
then providence moves too.

All sorts of things occur to help you
that would never otherwise have occurred.

A whole stream of events
derives from the decision,
raising in your favour all manner of unforeseen incidents
and meetings and material assistance,
which no one could have dreamt
would have come your way.
Author Unknown

Nelson Mandela: Inaugural Speech, 1994

Our deepest fear is not that we are inadequate.
Our deepest fear is that we are powerful beyond measure.
It is our light, not our darkness that most frightens us.

We ask ourselves,
Who am I to be brilliant,
gorgeous, talented, fabulous?
Actually, who are you *not* to be?

You are a child of God.
Your playing small does not serve the world.
There is nothing enlightened about shrinking,
So that other people won't feel insecure around you.
We are all meant to shine, as children do.

We were born to make manifest the glory of God that is
within us.
It is not just in some of us;
It's in everyone.
And as we let our own light shine,
We unconsciously give other people permission to do
the same.

As we are liberated from our own fear, our presence
automatically liberates others.

The Rose Still Grows Beyond The Wall

Near a shady wall a rose once grew,
Budded and blossomed in God's free light,
Watered and fed by morning dew,
Shedding its sweetness day and night.

As it grew and blossomed fair and tall,
Slowly rising to loftier height,
It came to a crevice in the wall,
Through which there shone a beam of light.

Onward it crept with added strength
With never a thought of fear or pride.
It followed the light through the crevice length
And unfolded itself on the other side.

The light, the dew, the broadening view
Were found the same as they were before;
And it lost itself in beauties new,
Breathing its fragrance more and more.

Shall claim of death cause us to grieve,
And make our courage faint or fall?
Nay, let us faith and hope receive:
The rose still grows beyond the wall.

Scattering fragrance far and wide,
Just as it did in days of yore,
Just as it did on the other side,
Just as it will forevermore.
A.L. Frink

About the Authors

Imelda Kelly-Butler

Imelda was inspired to write and compile this book, *Be Not Afraid ... I Go Before You*, following the sudden death of her husband John, caused by a wasp sting in July 2010. More than fifty people have contributed to the writing of the book, through their contributions of stories, their personal support and their encouragement throughout the process.

Imelda is Managing Director of Century Management which is a strategic change management company working with individuals, teams and businesses – helping them move from where they are to where they want to go, through developing a purpose, vision, strategy and competencies within their businesses.

Imelda's purpose and passion is to inspire individuals, teams and businesses to identify, clarify and fulfil their purpose in life and business.

Imelda is also Chairperson of Odyssey Transformational Strategies, an international consultancy organisation focused on working with consultants and corporate global clients worldwide.

A native of County Wicklow, Imelda and John have two wonderful daughters, Michelle and Maria. She lives in Forenaughts, Kill, Co Kildare where she participates in the local community.

There are a number of contributors who wish to maintain the anonymity of their name and the names of their dear, beloved ones. We acknowledge, respect and appreciate the work of all authors / contributors to the book.

Contact: Imelda K Butler
Email: imeldabutler@centurymanagement.ie
Telephone: 00 353 1 4595950
Mobile: 00 353 86 2606077

LIST OF CONTRIBUTORS
Appearing alphabetically by First Name

<u>Name</u>   <u>Category</u>   <u>Title</u>   <u>Page</u>

Name	Category	Title	Page
Agnes Young	Parent	*Cherry Blossom Petal*	48
Anna Melia	Parent	*A Walk In My Shoes*	68
Bernie O'Reilly	Partner	*Learning to Live ...*	28
Bill	Partner	*Finding a Place ...*	41
Brian	Sibling	*Suicide to a Sibling*	93
Brian Carthy	Sibling	*A Flickering Candle*	88
Bridget Critchley	Partner	*Getting My Peace Back*	44
Carol Renaud Gaffney	Children	*Last Lessons*	196
Daphne Wright	Children	*His Presence Is Beside Me ...*	177
David Wright	Friend	*My Neighbours & Male Friends*	124
Debbie Baker	Children	*Unconditional Love*	228
Diana Chipo Munanairi	Children	*Mr Africa – Living Through Me*	168
Elaine Gagne	Children	*Fly Away, Jean*	190
Frances Wiley	Friend	*Death ends a life ...*	110
Geoffrey Steinemann	Children	*Succisa Virescit*	173
Gerard Healion	Children	*It's Nice to Be Nice ...*	155
Geraldine Buckley	Partner	*A Broken Open-Heart ...*	21
Hasan Hahsin Güngör	Children	*My First Step To Maturity*	193
Helen Jackson	Sibling	*At Peace & Rest: Our ...*	98
Hubert Hopkins	Children	*The Strength Losing ...*	184
Imelda K Butler	Partner	*A Great Life & Partnership ...*	12
Jane Hamilton	Children	*Our Mum – A Very Special Lady*	223
Jim Redmond & Alice	Partner	*Treasured Memories of Lou*	31
John Oakes	Children	*The Swaying Barley Stalks*	179
Karen Benz	Children	*Gifts in Times of Sorrow*	182
Kathy	Partner	*Things Seem Better in the Light*	35
Kyla Bonnstetter	Sibling	*Beautiful & Free At Last*	90
Larry Gogan	Partner	*Florrie My Soul Mate ...*	17
Len Wiley	Children	*My Gratitude to My Mum*	205
Linda Anker Belle	Parent	*The Ebb & Flow of a Life*	77

GRÁ Foundation

In rural Kenya, I saw death – I thought of grief. I realised that grief is universal. I saw smiles – I thought of happiness. Happiness is universal. I felt the love in homes. Love is universal. But the difference is that children in Kenya do not always have food. Food is not universal. Education and basic needs are not universal in our world.

Maria Butler, Founder of GRÁ (Growth Reaching Africa), speaking of her first experience in Kenya.

This book is filled with stories of sadness and loss. Yet there is an equal amount of love and hope to be found in the same stories. We named our initiative GRÁ (meaning love in Gaelic/Irish) because the focus is on making a positive and meaningful difference in rural Kenya, by investing in education and development. My father, John Butler, who passed away suddenly in 2010 and is the inspiration for this book, was a key supporter, advocate and believer in GRÁ. He was an enthusiastic participant in the GRÁ sponsorship programme.

GRÁ is an initiative that invests in the education and development of young people, families and communities in rural Kenya. GRÁ focuses on learning, empowerment, promoting human dignity and the connection between people. GRÁ was founded by Maria Butler and a group of friends and family with the aim of helping a few girls go to secondary school in a rural community. GRÁ has improved the lives of not only those girls but of thousands more through education, feeding and community development.

GRÁ has several projects in Kenya including: GRÁ Feeding Programmes; GRÁ Education Programmes; Community Development and Growth; Water Projects and Volunteer Workcamps. GRÁ Feeding Programmes operate in four primary schools and are vital as food, insecurity and rising food prices threaten life in rural Kenya.

The GRÁ Education Programme continues to expand. Through our Secondary and Third-level Scholarship Programmes, we sponsor young girls and boys to attend and complete secondary school and to progress to third-level university. GRÁ runs Growth Projects including employment schemes, construction projects and community development initiatives. Community participation and cross learning are the cornerstones to GRÁ's partnerships in Kenya.

Thank you for supporting this book filled with stories of GRÁ and for helping our projects in the rural communities of Kenya,

Maria Butler
Founder and Chair of GRÁ Charity
Read more about our work at: www.gracharity.com

Further Reading

Bozarth, Alla Renee, *A Journey Through Grief: Gentle, Specific Help to Get You Through the Most Difficult Stages of Grieving*, April, 1994.

Butler, John, *Crossing the Rubicon: Seven Steps to Writing Your Own Personal Strategy*, September, 2006.

Carrig, Janice, *A Holy Presence*.

Delaney, Susan, *Irish Stories of Loss and Hope*, April, 2007.

De Mello, Anthony, *Awareness*, March, 1997.

Mackey, Noreen, *Free at Last: An Introduction to Prayer and the Spiritual Life*, March, 2010.

Hicks, Esther & Jerry, *Getting Into The Vortex: Guided Meditations CD and User Guide*, 15 November 2010.

Keane, Colm, *Going Home: Irish Stories from the Edge of Death, Near-death Journeys, Out-of-body Travel, Death-bed Visions*, October, 2009.

Kenneally, Christy, *Life After Loss: Helping the Bereaved*, December, 1999.

Kübler-Ross, Elisabeth & Kessler, David, *On Grief and Grieving: Finding the Meaning of Grief Through the Five Stages of Loss*, June, 2007.

Kübler-Ross, Elisabeth, *Death: The Final Stage*, June, 1997.

Kübler-Ross, Elisabeth, *Living with Death and Dying*, June, 1997.

Lawton, Liam, *Hope Prayer*, October, 2010.

Leckey, Dolores R, *Grieving With Grace: A Woman's Perspective (Called to Holiness)*, August, 2008.

McCormack, Jerusha, *Grieving: A Beginner's Guide*, 2005.

McMahon, Paddy, *There Are No Goodbyes: Guided By Angels – My Tour of the Spirit World*, September, 2011.

Melia, Anna, *A Walk in My Shoes*, October, 2010.

Quinn, John, *Sea of Love, Sea of Loss*, June, 2003.

Wilson, Joan, *All Shall Be Well – A Bereavement Anthology and Companion*, June, 2008.